Growing Up Moral:
Dilemmas for the Intermediate Grades

# Growing Up Moral: Dilemmas for the Intermediate Grades

by Peter Scharf, William McCoy, and Diane Ross

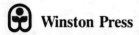 **Winston Press**

# Acknowledgments

Special thanks to Miriam Frost, Amy Rood, and
Pamela Espeland for their countless loving hours.

Library of Congress Catalog Card Number: 78-50391
ISBN: 0-03-043941-8
Printed in the United States of America

5  4  3  2

Winston Press, Inc.
430 Oak Grove
Minneapolis, MN 55403

For Doris, Adria, and Sage;
and for Barbara and Erin.

# Table of Contents

## Chapter IV
## Moral Dilemmas: A Workbook

## Appendix

## Bibliography—177

## Index of Dilemmas—182

# Chapter I
# An Introduction to Developmental Moral Education

# Sandy Curtis's Dilemma

The first thing Sandy Curtis thought about when he woke up on Monday morning was that he was facing a serious problem. Last week, Mr. Watkins, the Assistant Principal, had assigned Sandy to the school safety patrol. "You've earned this privilege by being one of the most responsible boys in the school," Mr. Watkins had said. It would be Sandy's job to help the kindergarten and first-grade children across a busy street, and he'd get to wear a white safety badge. Sandy was also captain of the Sixteenth Street punchball team, and that was part of his problem. He was supposed to start on the safety patrol that afternoon—and his team was playing their championship game at the same time.

Sandy had been a member of his block's punchball team for as long as he could remember, and now that he was captain it was even more important for him to show up at every game. The evening before, Billy Rodriquez had asked him how many runs he was going to score. "Seven," Sandy had said proudly, rolling up his sleeves to show his muscles. Sandy also remembered what Donny Sutton had once said about the safety patrol: "Safety's just another word for sissy."

Mr. Watkins was counting on him to report for the safety patrol on Monday afternoon. If he was late—or if he didn't show up at all—the little kids wouldn't have anyone to help them cross the street. Tommy, Sandy's five-year-old brother, was so excited that Sandy had been chosen safety patroller that he could barely stop talking long enough to eat his cereal. All during breakfast, Tommy rattled on about how *his* brother would get to wear a white badge and tell all the other kids what to do. "You really gonna do it?" he asked excitedly. "That'll be something! I can't wait till my friends see you!"

Sandy wondered how he was going to be in two places at the same time, helping the kids cross the street and playing punchball with his team. He hardly touched his breakfast.

"Forty-two to thirteen!" his father grumbled into the sports section when Sandy tried to get his attention. "They oughta fire the coach. The Giants haven't done anything since they traded Sam Huff. . . ." Sandy's mother wasn't much help, either. She was worried about Sandy's baby sister. "Sara's cold is worse, and I'll need the car today to take her to the doctor," she said to Sandy's dad. She didn't really hear what Sandy said.

Sandy left for school early and thought about his problem all the way there. He barely noticed his friend Alex, and he forgot to thank Mr. Sullivan at the store where he bought a notebook. After crossing Broadway, Sandy decided that he'd talk to his homeroom teacher, Ms. Snow. She was nice. She never yelled at anyone in the class, and she always seemed to understand how sixth-grade kids felt. Sandy knew that she usually got to school early enough to have a cup of coffee and a muffin.

As he stopped at the door of Ms. Snow's room, Sandy saw that she was reading a book and looked like she was thinking hard. She was holding a coffee cup in one hand and a muffin in the other. She looked up as he walked in.

"Hi, Sandy," she said. "You're early!"

"Hi, Ms. Snow," Sandy answered.

"What's up?"

"Oh, nothing—well, almost nothing."

"What's almost nothing?" she asked, putting her coffee cup down. She marked her place in her book and waited for Sandy to go on.

"Well. . .," Sandy began. "You see, I told Mr. Watkins that I would work on the safety patrol this afternoon, and I also told Billy Rodriguez and some of my other friends that I'd play on our punchball team in the championship game today. I'm the captain. That game starts after school, too. I can't patrol and play in the game at the same time! And my little brother thinks it's great that I'm gonna help him and his friends cross the street, and my mother was so proud of me that she already told my Aunt Sophie, and the other guys on the punchball team are gonna be really mad if I don't show up, and they might not let me be captain anymore . . . and I don't know what to do! What do *you* think I should do?"

Although Sandy Curtis's problem isn't particularly earthshaking, it's certainly important to him. Sandy is facing a *moral dilemma* which presents him with a number of confusing questions. His eleven-year-old mind is probably swimming with contradictions. Mr. Watkins is counting on him. His punchball team is counting on him. Donny Sutton thinks safety patrolling is for sissies, but Sandy's mother and little brother are very proud that Sandy's been picked to do it. Which promise is more important—the one he made to Mr. Watkins or the one he made to his team? Who comes first, and why? Someone's going to be mad at him, that's for sure—but who?

Elementary school children face moral issues like this one each and every day, even though they and the adults around them may not recognize the fact that seemingly commonplace situations are often moral dilemmas. It's critical that children learn to confront these dilemmas if they're to grow into morally responsible adults. This ongoing process of encountering moral conflicts and making decisions about them is what *Growing Up Moral* is about. And we're the Ms. Snows that children like Sandy are coming to for advice.

What's our responsibility? How can we help these children? Whether we like it or not, we're faced with our students' dilemmas as squarely as they themselves are. How we choose to work with the children and their problems can significantly affect the kinds of persons they become. We can tell them what to do in no uncertain terms and leave it at that. We can let them make up their own minds and try to be around when they err. We can ignore them and hope that their families are providing them with a healthy, nurturing environment that will aid them in making the right decisions. We can shelve their problems to be considered later, when we're not so busy ourselves. Or we can work to familiarize ourselves with real and usable techniques to help children like Sandy make the best decisions possible and learn from those decisions.

## Cognitive Moral Development Theory

Cognitive moral development theory can aid us in understanding the moral conflicts children meet in their everyday lives. The three words which name the theory also begin to define it. *Cognitive* refers to the organized thought processes which come into play whenever a child must make a moral decision. *Moral* refers to decision making in situations where ethical values conflict—is it *ever* right to lie, or steal, or tattle on a friend? *Development* suggests that patterns of thinking and perceptions about moral issues evolve *qualitatively* over time.[1] *Growing Up Moral* presents a practical overview of the theory of cognitive moral development as it applies to the moral education of the elementary school child. It provides a series of dilemmas which can be used to explore and implement the theory. And it shows how the theory can be applied to the growing pains of children like Sandy as we help them to become morally aware and responsible human beings.

Like any theory, cognitive moral development has its history. Developmental psychologists Jean Piaget and Lawrence Kohlberg have played particularly important roles in helping us to gain insight into children's thinking and moral development. Both Piaget and Kohlberg offer some very useful ways of looking at the real-life dilemmas which elementary school children like Sandy often face and guide us in understanding and anticipating their responses as we encourage them to grow morally. (See the appendix on page 175 for a chart comparing the Piaget and Kohlberg stages of development.)

## Piaget's Theory of Logical Development

Jean Piaget was one of the first modern philosophers to systematically document the fact that the child views his or her world in a way quite different from that of adults. According to Piaget, the child's view of reality evolves in terms of his or her increasing awareness of both natural and social phenomena. Basically, Piaget's theory holds three central tenets:

1. Children have their own unique physical and social philosophies about the natural and social world.
2. These philosophies evolve in a sequence of *stages* which appear in all societies in the same order.
3. The higher stages provide more comprehensive and accurate ways of seeing and responding to reality than earlier, less mature stages do.

Piaget called the first era of logical development—from birth to age two—the *sensory-motor* stage. A young person at this stage has not yet discovered that objects exist once they're out of sight. When a ball leaves a child's field of vision, the child believes that the ball has disappeared. And when Mommy leaves the room, the child is convinced that Mommy has disappeared, too, and may holler about it.

At roughly age two, the child develops what Piaget terms *symbolic, intuitive,* or *preoperational* thought. At this stage, symbols become real. A teddy bear is not simply a lump of cloth; rather, it becomes a symbolic being to the child, a friend who needs to be fed, nurtured, and cared for. At this point in his or her development, a child frequently confuses reality and make-believe. The Mickey Mouse man at Disneyland, for example, is still seen as the real Mickey Mouse even after he's removed his mask.

At approximately ages five through seven, the child's orientation toward reality begins to change again. Piaget refers to this phase of development as the period of *concrete operations.* During this time, the child develops the ability to think about what's real and what isn't according to fixed, rule-bound ways of ordering reality. He or she becomes more objective. Reality is distinguished from appearance. Now when the Mickey Mouse man removes his mask, he is no longer Mickey Mouse to the child.

The transition to *formal operational* thought comes next. At this stage, the preadolescent or adolescent begins to coherently and systematically weigh logical propositions and consider alternatives. He or she is also able to reflect on his or her own thoughts. Surprisingly, some adults don't manage to reach this final stage of development; research has shown that roughly 40 percent of all adults remain at the *concrete operational* stage throughout their lives.

## Piaget's Theory of Moral Development

Piaget's theory holds that moral thinking develops in a sequence similar to that of logical thinking. During the 1930s, Piaget conducted one of his most imaginative studies; it had to do with how children's perceptions of rules change over time. While observing and interviewing children from different parts of Switzerland, Piaget found three unique conceptions of the rules for a game of marbles.

He discovered that the rules used by children below the age of six were almost totally *egocentric.* Paralleling the preoperational stage, these children imitated aspects of the rules followed by older children without really understanding or adhering to them.

Another example of this type of reasoning was observed recently in America. A five-year-old boy was playing baseball with some older children. He purposefully grabbed the bat, taking the stance of the major leaguers he'd watched. When, after eleven swings, he finally managed to hit the ball, he proceeded to run directly toward the pitcher (who happened to be his brother) to say hello. After being guided to first base, he leaned forward in good imitation of a player about to steal second. But as the next batter hit the ball, the child sat down on the base and called it a "pretty chair."

This egocentric stage is followed by what Piaget terms the stage of *moral heteronomy* (ages six through ten). Paralleling the stage of concrete operations, children now look upon rules as sacred and unchangeable. They feel that rules are right in and of themselves simply because they're rules. Piaget observed that children at this stage obeyed rules for their game of marbles to the letter even if the rule didn't work or was meaningless. Apparently, the children perceived rules as if imposed by an external order and demanding obedience.

Finally, parallel to the formal operational stage (about ages eleven and up) is what Piaget calls the stage of *moral autonomy*. To children at this point in their lives, rules are intentional and created for everybody's benefit—which means that they're subject to change. Adolescent children playing stickball in the streets, for example, will adjust their rules when a manhole is uncovered or when a car which used to be third base is suddenly driven off. Because these children are becoming more flexible, they no longer need to settle social conflicts by appeals to authority. ("I'll tell on you if you don't stop.") Instead, they resolve conflicts by considering the common good. ("Stop fighting or you'll ruin the game for all of us.")

An understanding of the "revolution" in preadolescent thinking—from concrete operations toward formal operations—has numerous implications for the upper elementary school teacher. First, it's critical to realize that preadolescents see the world in a much different way than younger children and adults do. They're often "in-between" many things, and this can be confusing to the teacher. The child's new self-consciousness should be understood not as mere silliness or purely a product of biological maturity, but rather as evidence of a fresh consciousness and intellectual outlook. The teacher who keeps this in mind can make sense out of a child's unusual or apparently unrelated answers to questions. For example, the child who says that "George Washington was worried about having too many soldiers killed because he wanted his army to like him" (Rachel, age eleven) can be understood as describing Washington's motives according to her own frame of reference.

Second, it's also important to keep reminding oneself that the range of intellectual development in preadolescents is very great (as, of course, is the range of physical development). Some students in an average sixth-grade class may still be at the concrete operational stage, while others may be in transition and still others may be capable of full formal operations. This range has obvious implications for both teaching and counseling. School tasks and classwork should be developed to match the children's cognitive abilities as closely as possible. It's often easy to assume that all elementary children have intellectual abilities that they in fact do *not* have. For example, teachers commonly ask inferential questions that are far beyond the capacity of their students to understand or answer. If a fifth-grade teacher approaches a unit on the Civil War by asking students to pick the most important cause of the war (such as economic, racial, or political forces), he or she will find that few of the students are capable of weighing the complex variables implied by the question.

Third, knowledge of the developmental stages can help us to determine goals for education which transcend in importance the mastery of a particular subject matter. Viewed in this way, the goal of the elementary school is to stimulate a wide range of intellectual operations. In moving the child toward formal operations, the school seeks to offer the child a truly scientific and objective view of both physical and social realities.

Finally, the child's conception of moral ideas and social relationships depends, at least in part, on his or her ability to intellectually resolve interpersonal conflicts. The responsibility for teaching these skills, as well as for allowing opportunities to apply them in the context of ongoing relationships, is in large part placed upon the elementary school teacher and the school, whether we like it or not. Understanding how a child *reasons* morally can help us to guide him or her.

## Kohlberg's Theory of Moral Development

Piaget was the first modern psychologist to scientifically observe that the child's conception of social rules evolves in stages. His work served as a starting point for Lawrence Kohlberg, a psychologist-educator from Harvard University. For the past twenty-five years, Kohlberg has documented that moral ideas evolve in an invariant sequence which is the same in every society. According to Kohlberg, this sequence always moves in the direction of a more comprehensive, rational, *ethical* philosophy.

Kohlberg has found that moral judgment progresses through a never-changing series of *six stages*. His theory, like Piaget's, makes three fundamental claims:

1. First, the six stages form a universal invariant sequence; that is, they progress in the same order regardless of surrounding circumstances. Thus, Stage 3 must always follow Stage 2, Stage 4 must always follow Stage 3, and so on—in spite of society, subculture, or historical age.[2]
2. Second, each stage must possess what Piaget calls a psychological whole;[3] that is, each stage must describe a complete theory of moral and social relationships.
3. Finally, each stage must be defined as being more philosophically *adequate* than earlier stages are; that is, each higher stage must define a more coherent and rational way of resolving moral conflict than any preceding stage does.

Kohlberg terms the first two of the six stages *preconventional.* Each of these stages involves a *physical* conception of morality. At Stage 1, the *punishment-and-obedience* orientation (roughly ages six and seven), the child decides whether an action is good or bad, right or wrong, on the basis of its physical consequences. If something is punished, it's wrong; if a child does something that Mommy yells about, it's wrong. On the other hand, if an action is accepted by an authority figure, it's right.

At Stage 2, the *instrumental-relativist* orientation (roughly ages eight through ten), "right" action is that which satisfies one's own needs and occasionally the needs of others. Human relationships are viewed in terms of the marketplace: "You scratch my back, and I'll scratch yours." The child is beginning to perceive elements of fairness, reciprocity, and sharing, but they're always interpreted in physical, pragmatic terms. He or she has little or no consideration yet for loyalty, gratitude, or justice.

The *conventional* level, which includes Stages 3 and 4, usually becomes dominant in late preadolescence. At this level, maintaining the rules, expectations, and standards of the family group, peer group, or nation is all important, regardless of immediate or obvious consequences. The child is concerned not only with conforming to the social order, but also with maintaining, justifying, and supporting that order.

At Stage 3, the *interpersonal concordance* or "good boy/good girl" orientation (beginning at about age ten), good behavior is seen as that which helps others and is condoned by them. A child gains approval by being "nice" or by behaving in ways that are accepted by others. Right is defined by what others expect, and behavior is often judged by intentions; "he means well" or "it's the thought that counts" are seen as reasonable for the first time.

At Stage 4, the *law-and-order* orientation (beginning in early adolescence), a person's consciousness shifts toward fixed definitions of social duty, concern with rules, and a respect for formal authority. Right is defined by doing one's duty. A person at this stage recognizes that laws and other social institutions serve clear purposes and are justified both for their own sake and because they maintain the social order.

The *postconventional, autonomous,* or *principled* level of moral development, encompassing Stages 5 and 6, usually begins in late adolescence and is characterized by an awareness of and actions based on autonomous moral principles. These principles are seen as having validity apart from the authority of the group or individuals in power. The principled thinker is able to evaluate the moral validity of concrete social rules and norms by comparing them with more general ideals of justice and fairness.

Stage 5, the *social-contract, legalistic* orientation, generally has utilitarian overtones. Law is perceived as having a basis in consent and in the welfare of people rather than simply in a respect for authority, as at Stage 4. Laws which aren't consitutional, which violate human rights, or which aren't in the general interest are judged invalid.

Finally, Kohlberg suggests that at Stage 6, the *universal-ethical-principle* orientation, a basis exists for rational agreement with moral principles. Right is defined by *ethical principles* which appeal to logical consistency, comprehensiveness, and universality. The principles held at this stage are abstract and ethical instead of concrete and inflexible. They include universal principles of justice, ideal reciprocity, the equality of human rights, and the respect for the dignity of human beings as *individual persons.*

# Changes in the Preadolescent's Intelligence

According to Piaget and Kohlberg, dramatic changes occur both in a preadolescent's reasoning ability and in his or her *moral and social outlook.* Let's examine changes in reasoning ability first.

As developmental psychologists define it, intelligence means much more than IQ: Intelligence also implies the way in which a child orders and understands his or her physical and social world. The key transformation in intelligence during preadolescence is from a *concrete operational* to a *formal operational* concept of problem solving. At the concrete operational stage, the child sees the world as stable. The differences between right and wrong are clear, and everything operates according to well-defined principles. Explanations offered by children of certain events tend to be logical and coherent but rather simple—a bank robber is bad, a police officer is good. If a baseball team loses a game, it's often because of a single reason: The team made mistakes, or it was their unlucky day, or they didn't try hard enough. Favorite school activities and exercises are usually those which have concrete, unarguable answers. Most early preadolescents, for example, enjoy matching state capitals to states, doing computation problems, and compiling facts, because there are "right" answers to these problems.

The transformation to formal operational thought is a dramatic one. Instead of considering only single explanations of phenomena or single solutions to problems, children begin to weigh possibilities and to select from a number of alternatives. They begin to be able to judge friends, relatives, and peers from vantage points other than their own. Instead of thinking that Billy *is* a stinker, a child at this stage will begin to understand that some people may *think* that Billy is a stinker, but that this doesn't make it a fact. Ideologies and philosophies become important for the first time. In school, tasks which have a number of possible solutions instead of just one become easier to understand and more enjoyable; for example, children at this stage might be enthusiastic about designing a make-believe city for the year 2000.

The move from concrete to formal operations is, of course, a gradual one; in fact, it is one of the central tasks of preadolescence. It requires that the preadolescent child radically shift his or her perspective on the world. Not only is the child's conception of physical reality altered, but his or her conception of both self and others changes as well. One dramatic aspect of the shift toward formal operations is the child's increased self-consciousness. David Elkind refers to this as the onset of "preadolescent egocentrism."[4] The girl who a year earlier was outgoing and concerned mostly with the world of play and the daily routines of life suddenly becomes almost obsessed with how other people see her. While going to a party at age ten implies seeing friends, eating cake, and playing new games, it becomes at age twelve a social ritual at which the child suddenly feels as if he or she is on display. One twelve year old described a party she "had to go to" as follows:

> Well, I know that Billy will be there and he might not like the way I look. And if I don't have lots of people to talk to, then the other kids will think that I'm not popular.

Although this sudden "preadolescent egocentrism" may be a great burden for the older elementary-school child, it is, in large part, a product of cognitive growth toward formal operational thought. For the first time, the child is able to see the world from an intellectual perspective other than his or her own. A child at this stage knows that other people are aware of and react to his or her ideas, attitudes, and mannerisms. The hard realism of concrete operational thought becomes a thing of the past. The new interpersonal world is one of conflicting attitudes, value systems, and beliefs. This transition phase is, of course, frustrating for many preadolescents (and their parents and teachers), but it's a necessary step toward becoming a mature adult.

# The Moral Reasoning of the Preadolescent Child

Paralleling the transformations in a child's reasoning ability are a series of equally dramatic changes in his or her conception of the nature of right and wrong. According to Kohlberg, moral reasoning progresses through a sequence of six stages, each stage more philoscphically adequate than the previous one. During the upper elementary years, children generally move through each of the first three stages—Stage 1, the punishment-and-obedience orientation; Stage 2, the instrumental-relativist orientation ("You scratch my back, and I'll scratch yours"); and Stage 3, the interpersonal concordance or "good boy/good girl" orientation. To illustrate these changes, let's look in detail at two children named Jeff and Judy, each of whom was interviewed three times between the ages of six and twelve. Both children were judged by their teacher to be of average maturity. Each was told the following story of Heinz* and his sick wife and asked if it would be right to steal a drug from an extorting druggist if one's wife were dying of a disease that the drug might cure.

> A woman who lived in Europe was near death. She had a very bad disease, a rare form of cancer that the doctors knew nothing about. There was, however, one drug that the doctors thought might save her. A druggist who lived in the same town as the dying woman had recently discovered the drug. It was expensive to make, since radium was a necessary ingredient, but even so the druggist was charging ten times what the drug cost him to make. He paid two hundred dollars for the radium and charged two thousand dollars for a very small dose of the drug. Heinz, the sick woman's husband, went to everyone he knew in an attempt to borrow enough money to buy some of the drug for his wife, but he could get together only about a thousand dollars. He told the druggist that his wife was dying and asked him to either sell the drug more cheaply or let him pay for it later. But the druggist refused, saying, "I discovered the drug, and I'm going to make as much money from it as I can." Heinz finally got so desperate that he broke into the druggist's store to steal the drug.

> When Jeff was asked at age six, "Would you steal the drug?" he answered,
> No, because stealing is against the law. Heinz could go to jail. *He would get into trouble.*

Jeff clearly demonstrated Stage 1 reasoning, focusing on the punishment which would be the consequence of stealing: "He would get into trouble."

*adapted from one of the dilemmas used in Kohlberg's original research.

When Jeff was interviewed three years later, he offered a justification *for* stealing:
> He could steal the drug, because *his wife is real important to him.* He would want her to live.

Jeff exhibited a Stage 2 rationale that stealing is OK when it is useful for one's own interests: "His wife is real important to him." When Jeff was asked what he'd do if he didn't like his wife, he argued as if his obligation to steal would be based on his objective relationship with his wife rather than any affectional tie:
> Well, I'd let her die; *but* if he did let her die then he'd have something over him all his life. He should get a divorce and *then* let her die.

By age twelve, Jeff had matured toward a Stage 3 attitude, focusing on the expectations of others in the community towards stealing:
> I don't think he should have stole. He could have gotten money somewhere else. But if he got caught, *the jury would understand. He was just a husband trying to do what a husband should do*—if he was truly concerned and sincerely loved his wife.

When asked, "What should Heinz do if he doesn't love his wife?" Jeff answered,
> They're still married. I think he'd love her.

Judy's moral development was similar to Jeff's in terms of the *reasoning process;* however, she made entirely different decisions about the dilemma itself. At age five, while Jeff was using Stage 1 reasoning to explain why he *would not* steal, Judy used the same sort of reasoning to explain why she *would:*
> I would steal the drug. If I didn't, her parents would yell at me because she died.

At age nine, Judy reversed herself and said that it would be wrong to steal. She offered reasons quite similar to those Jeff used while he was *supporting* the idea of stealing the drug:
> He shouldn't steal. If he went to jail, it would be hard for her kids to live. Two people would be gone. The kids would be much harder up.

At age twelve, she took a rather similar Stage 3 point of view to that expressed by Jeff but again arrived at a different conclusion:

> Even though it would be wrong, because *people would say* it's against the law, he should steal it. He really cared about his wife, and *people would understand* why he did it.

A comparison of the two cases is very revealing. First, the process of reasoning evolved in each child from a rather primitive punishment-and-obedience orientation to one emphasizing reciprocal exchange and then progressed further to a position showing awareness of a morality of shared expectations. Second, the content of both children's responses shifted back and forth during the six-year period. Each child indicated at one point that he or she believed stealing was wrong and then asserted the opposite in a later interview. These developmental trends indicate that while children's opinions may oscillate in terms of specific issues, the evolution of their *reasoning* is invariant.

Let's look at some more responses to the Heinz dilemma. This time, we'll also discuss higher-stage responses in order to put the lower-stage responses into perspective.

When Jennifer, age five, was asked if Heinz should steal the drug, her response was typical of a Stage 1 orientation. (Again, this stage is characterized by extreme concreteness. Justice is determined by what a powerful person demands of a weaker one.) Jennifer replied,

> It would be wrong to take it. That's stealing. Stealing is wrong, and the policeman would see him do it and put him in jail.

When asked how she would feel if the sick woman was her mother, Jennifer said,

> It's stealing anyway. I don't want to go to jail. Does this place have a kids' jail?

Bob, age ten, gave a Stage 2 response indicating self-interest:

> I would probably steal it. If Heinz needed his wife, he should take it. It might be worth it for him to have his wife, even if he goes to jail.

Stage 3 or 4 conventional reasoning assumes a far more social stance than seen at preconventional Stages 1 and 2. A person at Stage 3 shows a clear awareness of the attitudes of society-at-large toward specific actions. For example, twelve-year-old Bill responded to the dilemma by saying,

> It would be very wrong to steal the drug. People would feel that Heinz was a thief and wouldn't speak to him.

At Stage 4, stealing is perceived as a violation of the law and a threat to the social order. Fifteen-year-old Tanya offers,

> It's a matter of the law. It's one of our rules, and we're trying to protect people and property. It's needed by society. We can't live without rules. Even though Heinz cares for his wife, he shouldn't steal.

The postconventional thinker at Stage 5 or 6 looks at moral problems in a way quite different from that of a person at an earlier, less developed stage. Instead of defining moral problems from the perspective of a member of a particular group or society, the postconventional, principled thinker views them from the perspective of universal rights, contracts, and obligations. For example, twenty-four-year-old Joe argues,

> The rights of the druggist should not have taken priority over those of the woman. What's really important here is a life. While the man should try all legal means to get the drug, it would be right to steal if—and only if—a life was at stake.

Kohlberg and his associates have suggested that each moral stage requires a particular capacity for logical thinking. Just because someone is able to *think* logically, however, does *not* imply that he or she will *act* morally. Attaining a specific logical stage doesn't ensure attainment of a comparable moral stage. Many individuals who are capable of abstract or formal operational thought (Piaget's highest stage) are morally primitive. For example, a person may be intellectually capable of creating a complicated device and be willing to use it for a destructive purpose. An educational system which has separated technical from moral education has, perhaps, created an unnecessary *decalage* (a gap in operations in different realms) in many adults who then operate with scientific logic in technical areas while still thinking in immature moral categories.

# How Moral Ideas Change

Kohlberg's research suggests that children's moral ideas change not simply because people teach them "good" moral values but rather because they're challenged in a number of different ways to think more deeply about moral problems. The environment in which a child lives has a lot to do with his or her rate of change and the final stage of moral thinking he or she is able to reach.

An important environmental condition which seems to be related to rapid and complete moral development involves the experience of *moral conflict,* or *disequilibrium,* and both the family and classroom can be sources of positive development in this area. A family that discusses moral issues together and challenges one another in a supportive yet questioning atmosphere is one which is likely to produce morally mature children. Even young children can respond to simple moral arguments. Let's say, for example, that you have a six year old who often yells loudly in the morning, waking up the rest of the family. Advancing an argument like, "If you try to be quiet in the morning when we're sleeping, we will try to be quiet during your favorite TV show" exposes your six year old to a Stage 2 sense of fair play and reciprocity.

*Empathy* is also an important factor in moral development. A family or classroom which encourages interpersonal understanding is likely to foster moral growth as well. Role taking and empathy are, in part, natural by-products of healthy social groups. A family or class which feels united and respects all members is often naturally empathetic; nevertheless, a parent or teacher can further encourage this process of mutual role taking. For example, if one child hits another, it might be useful to ask the first child, "How do you think Johnny felt when you hit him over the head?" Or, one might prompt the child to assume another's point of view by asking, "How would you feel if *you* were hit over the head?"

How *justice* is perceived in the family and school also relates to the development of moral thinking in the child. A parent or teacher who behaves in an arbitrary or inconsistent manner will be seen as unfair. Experiments conducted by Lawrence Kohlberg and Peter Scharf[5] indicate that prisons and school environments which are seen as being fair by inmates and students tend to encourage higher-stage moral thinking; in contrast, environments perceived as coercive or unfair tend to freeze their inhabitants at primitive stages of moral thought.

Finally, opportunities for *democratic dialogue* also seem to be related to advances in moral thinking. Institutions which encourage democratic interaction on the part of all students tend to foster moral thinking, while institutions which deny any form of democratic interchange tend to stunt the growth of moral thought. Orphanages (studied by Joan Thrower[6]) and reform schools (studied by Peter Scharf[7]) which actively discouraged any participation by their residents produced primitive moral thinkers. On the other hand, Joe Reimer[8] found that Israeli kibbutzum children, who are raised in an atmosphere where all persons are expected to participate in both work and governance from the age of six on, develop moral judgment at an accelerated pace.

Kohlberg's research indicates that children have great difficulty understanding moral ideas more than one stage above their own. For example, if a child with a Stage 3 orientation is asked to explain what a teacher means when she says that "all children in a democratic class are obliged to show mutual respect for all members in the class" (a Stage 5 remark), he or she might respond in this way:

> It means that we should be nice to everyone in the class or no one will like you.

Children tend to think harder about a moral dilemma—or, in other words, experience greater conflict—and to grow more when they're confronted with arguments one stage above their own. Arguments two or more stages above them simply aren't comprehensible to them. Arguments at a child's own stage are dismissed as being simple or obvious, while those below the child's own stage are rejected as being just plain silly. For example, a Stage 2 child who's told by a substitute teacher, "If you talk out of turn, you'll be sent to the principal's office" (a Stage 1 threat) might think,

> That's dumb; she probably won't send me, and anyway it's kind of nice in the principal's office. Everyone talks to you, and the secretary gives you drawing paper and crayons.

In other words, an environment which is trying to stimulate moral growth in a child should present him or her with moral reasoning one stage above the child's own.

# How Social Relationships Change

Parallel to changes in the elementary school child's moral judgment are equally important changes in his or her ideas about friendship. In his work with children, Robert Selman has found that the meaning of friendship evolves in a pattern that parallels the development of the moral stages and those of interpersonal role taking.[9] Friendships among children at Stage 1, for example, are conceived of in terms of uneven reciprocity. If a child is unhappy about the actions of a friend, he or she feels justified in terminating that friendship (at least temporarily):

> Becky wore a dumb dress to school today, so I don't like her anymore.

At Stage 2, friendships are seen as reciprocal relationships between two or more persons. Cooperation is necessary for the maintenance of a relationship, so lack of cooperation can easily cause a break in a friendship:

> Tommy and I like to play together, but when he doesn't want to roller-skate, I don't feel like playing with him.

At Stage 3, friendships are judged by what children expect of each other rather than by particular actions taken at particular times:

> Tom didn't ask me to play ball with him last Saturday, but we're still friends anyway.

Knowledge of these transformations in social thinking can help us understand many of the evolving social patterns evident during the elementary school years. Many researchers have noted the evolution of what Harry Stack Sullivan terms the "chum" and "clique" relationships.[10] Having a "chum" or a "buddy" (someone a child does everything with, goes everywhere with, and tells everything to) requires at least a Stage 2 conception of mutual exchange and reciprocity. One needs to be able to take the part of another—to empathize—in addition to understanding *how* a friendship meets the needs of both persons involved. Similarly, membership in a clique requires a Stage 3 perspective of "the group" as well as a conception of group mutuality. One needs to be able to understand that a group has attitudes in common and expects certain things of its members. An excerpt from the diary of an eleven-year-old girl offers a good example of the Stage 3 social world:

November 21, 19____
Dear Diary,

Sylvia wore a red dress today. Nancy thought it looked nice. I don't think Nancy liked my dress. It was green. Bobby talked to me during "Nutrition." (Oooh!) He's cute, like Shawn Cassidy. (Oooh!) I think that Nancy saw me talking to him. She looked Green with Envy. I hope Nancy will invite me to her party Saturday. She knows that Bobby wants me to come. I think that I'll get to go. Oh, yes—I hate my Reading teacher. He dresses weird. Everyone thinks he's weird. I also hate Gym. I look so weird in my tank suit. I hope Bobby never sees me in it! Till tomorrow. . .

## The Developmental Moral Educator's Approach to Sandy's Dilemma

Now that we've looked at Piaget's and Kohlberg's theories of intellectual and moral development, let's recall Sandy Curtis and his dilemma, found at the beginning of this chapter. How can Ms. Snow best help Sandy to handle his problem?

According to developmental theory, the teacher who wants to help a child reason through a moral dilemma has to be both a moral philosopher and a moral psychologist. The effective teacher must be able to define the probable ways in which a child sees a moral conflict and simultaneously to employ a strategy which could lead to further moral learning on the part of the child. If this sounds like a big job, it is. Any time a person makes a deliberate effort to advance the thinking of another, it's a big job—but it isn't by any stretch of the imagination an impossible one. Familiarity with certain techniques can make the developmental theory and its practice much more accessible and less intimidating. Basically, an understanding of cognitive moral development theory can be used to find reasonable, useful ways for a teacher to get in touch with his or her students and help them along.

The first thing Ms. Snow should do, *after* listening carefully to Sandy's description of his problem, is to try to understand the moral dilemma he faces—but from *his* point of view, not her own.

Developmental theory provides her with some tools for doing just that. It states that since Sandy is eleven years old, he's probably somewhere between Stages 2 and 3 in his moral development. *Probably* is a key word here. It's very important to avoid both labeling children according to the stages they're in at a particular time and having inflexible expectations of them from that point on. Furthermore, it's essential to keep in mind that each child is an individual and that no child will fit perfectly into the confines of any theory.

As we recall, Sandy described his problem as follows: "I told Mr. Watkins that I would work on the safety patrol this afternoon, and I also told Billy Rodriquez and some of my other friends that I'd play on our punchball team in the championship game today. I'm the captain. That game starts after school, too. I can't patrol and play in the game at the same time! And my little brother thinks it's great that I'm gonna help him and his friends cross the street, and my mother was so proud of me that she already told my Aunt Sophie, and the other guys on the punchball team are gonna be really mad if I don't show up, and they might not let me be captain anymore . . . and I don't know what to do! What do you think I should do?"

From Sandy's description of his dilemma, Ms. Snow can gauge the kinds of concerns *Sandy* sees as important in this conflict. For example, Sandy's concern that the guys on his team won't let him stay captain is a typical Stage 2 concern with Sandy's own instrumental needs. His concern about disappointing Mr. Watson and his mother is a Stage 3 response, an orientation to others' expectations. It's doubtful that Sandy is worried about either a Stage 4 duty to the safety patrol or the punchball team or about Stage 5 notions of formal contracts or commitments.

Developmental theory holds that the right decision in this situation isn't a matter of what society or the school thinks best, nor is it a matter of Sandy's immediate personal opinion. Rather, it's a matter of what's just and fair regardless of the standards of a particular society or group. If Sandy is to learn and grow morally as a result of this dilemma, it won't be because Ms. Snow *tells* him what to do or leaves him to wrestle with his own feelings but because she carries on a *dialogue* with him in a way that respects his opinions while stimulating him in the direction of a more mature moral thinking. Developmental theory emphasizes that if Ms. Snow helps Sandy work through his problem, Sandy might reach the most mature decision *he* is capable of making and grow morally at the same time.

This strategy implies the following two key assumptions:

1. that Sandy's position may be evaluated according to general principles of justice; and
2. that Sandy's ideas may evolve even further through a process of supportive intellectual challenge and dialogue.

Once Ms. Snow understands precisely how Sandy views the moral issues of his particular dilemma, she then might gradually question him in order to help him work through the dilemma. However, all during her discussion with Sandy, Ms. Snow must be aware that the issue at hand represents a *legitimate* conflict of claims between school, family, and peers and that each possible decision—to help the kids cross the street or to play punchball—has its valid reasons. Determining those reasons and helping Sandy make them morally sounder is Ms. Snow's responsibility at this point.

Sandy has said that the team will be mad if he doesn't show up and *that they might not let him be captain.* His reason for playing punchball, as pointed out earlier, represents a Stage 2 concern for his own desire to be captain. Now, Ms. Snow, focusing on the feelings of Sandy's teammates, might challenge Sandy in this way: "You said the guys would be mad if you didn't play. Why do you suppose they'd feel angry?" This question leads Sandy to some Stage 3 considerations: "I'm a good player, and they might lose without me. I guess I'd be mad, too." Or, "They elected me captain, so it wouldn't be very fair for me not to show up. I don't want them to think I'm finking out."

Sandy also gave reasons for joining the safety patrol: one, *my mother was so proud of me,* reflects a Stage 3 orientation to what others think of him. To this, Ms. Snow could inject a question which might lead Sandy to some Stage 4 considerations: "Why would being a safety patroller make your mom proud of you?" Sandy's possible thinking: "Well, the safety patrol is important. If the school didn't have one, the littler kids would be in danger." However, Sandy might as easily answer, "Mom'll be proud because I'll get to wear a badge." Sandy may not yet be capable of Stage 4 moral reasoning—if he's in transition between Stages 2 and 3. In that case, Ms. Snow should concentrate on helping him reach Stage 3 and reinforce his concern with what other people expect. "I'll bet your little brother and his friends will be proud, too." Ms. Snow has to keep her own position toward the dilemma in mind, as well, so she can answer honestly when Sandy asks her what *she* would do in the situation. She might reply:

> Well, Sandy, this is a tough one. I remember having to face a couple of problems like this one myself. I know how you feel about not wanting to disappoint the kids on your team, but I guess I think that making sure the little kids cross the street safely is more important right now. Besides, your little brother is really looking forward to seeing you wearing your badge. But that's just my opinion. What do *you* think you're going to do?

Naturally, these are hypothetical approaches, and the question-and-answer session might be much different under actual circumstances from the one we've proposed here. By definition, a moral dilemma has no right or wrong answers, no clearcut solution; according to Kohlberg, however, there may be some answers that are *better* than others or more "philosophically adequate," and Ms. Snow *can* help Sandy arrive at a decision that's sounder than one he might choose on his own. She *can* actively contribute to Sandy's moral development.

In order to be truly effective, however, moral education shouldn't have to depend on natural circumstances or dilemmas which occur spontaneously. If moral education is to become part of a classroom routine, it can't wait for dilemmas to happen. Besides, Sandy may have decided not to approach Ms. Snow for advice. Dilemmas don't have to occur spontaneously—they can, in a sense, be *manufactured* and used as tools to further moral education in the classroom. They can be found in history or science books, on the evening news, during play-acting. Where and how to find moral dilemmas will be discussed later.

## Implications

The studies and ideas discussed in this chapter can help us to understand the preadolescent child and to play an important role in his or her moral and social development. Keeping these findings in mind can give us a general idea of what to expect from children of this age and guide us in guiding them.

Elementary school children go through a series of radical transformations both in their ideas and actions. Their development of perceptions of right and wrong—and of what distinguishes one from the other—parallel the kinds of personal relationships in which they choose to engage. Children at this point in their development also go through dramatic changes in their intellectual, moral, and social lives—but each does so at a unique rate and deserves special consideration. In a single sixth-grade classroom, for example, a teacher might find children at the concrete operational stage as well as children who've entered the formal operational stage. In terms of Kohlberg's theory of moral development, some children might still be at Stage 1, while others will have reached higher stages—2 or 3. Similarly, children's social relationships will vary; some will form solely unilateral friendships—they'll have "chums" or "buddies" or "best friends"—while others will prefer the mutuality of clique relationships.

The changes in the preadolescent child's reasoning and in his or her perceptions of the world are evident not only in the kinds of relationships the child chooses, but also in the kinds of choices he or she makes in experimental and natural situations. Understanding the progression of moral, intellectual, and social reasoning during this period can provide us with a basis for gaining a deeper knowledge of the behavior of the preadolescent child; more importantly, it can also enable us to create an educational curriculum matched to the child's developmental needs.

This idea—of creating a curriculum to match our students' needs—deserves further examination. Elementary schools *could* actively aid in stimulating children's intellectual, moral, and social development, but unfortunately they too often don't. If we are to take seriously John Dewey's dictum that *development should be the aim of education,* then we must consider how the upper elementary school environment might best meet these goals.

One problem lies in the area of how educational goals are defined. Those of the elementary school are most often conceptualized in terms of basic literacy and adequate discipline. A more reasonable goal for elementary schools might be that of developing and applying the natural abilities unique to this age group to the children's social and moral needs. One way of doing this well is by creating moral dilemmas and other developmentally significant activities which are systematically matched both to the *moral stages* and to the *concerns* of preadolescent children. We might approach moral education, for example, by bringing up issues of emerging sexuality and peer friendship. And, by posing these issues in ways that are comprehensible to the stage 1, 2, and 3 students in our classrooms, we can be responsive to their concerns while at the same time using these concerns as the content of their moral education.

The ideas discussed above will be explored further in Chapter 2. In the meantime, the following brief overview of developmental theory should suggest a number of guidelines to keep in mind while teaching elementary school children.

1. First, young children's ideas about both the scientific and social world differ greatly from those of adults.
2. Second, the quality of the child's environment—both at school and in the home—influences the rate of moral development he or she experiences and the stage he or she eventually reaches as an adult. Basically, environments which stimulate moral conflict, encourage role taking, emphasize democratic interaction, and are seen by the children as being fair encourage accelerated moral development.
3. And finally, children in general have difficulty understanding moral arguments *more than one stage higher* than their own. Moral positions only one stage above the child's own, in general, create more positive moral conflict and more opportunities for growth than do positions either far above the child's stage of reasoning or below it. Further discussion of *developmental match* is given in Chapter 2.

## Notes

1. Lawrence Kohlberg, "The Cognitive-Developmental Approach to Moral Education," *Phi Delta Kappan* (June 1975): 670-77.
2. Lawrence Kohlberg, "Stage and Sequence: The Cognitive-Developmental Approach to Socialization," in *Handbook of Socialization Theory and Research,* ed. D.A. Goslin (Chicago: Rand McNally, 1969).

3. Lawrence Kohlberg, "From Is to Ought: How to Commit the Naturalistic Fallacy and Get Away with It in the Study of Moral Development," in *Cognitive Development and Epistemology,* ed. T. Mischel (New York: Academic Press, 1971).
4. David Elkind, *Children and Adolescents* (New York: Oxford University Press, 1972).
5. Peter Scharf and Joseph Hickey, *Towards a Just Community in Prison* (San Francisco: Jossey-Bass, 1979).
6. Joan Thrower, "Moral Reasoning among Institutionalized Orphan Children" (unpublished thesis, Harvard Graduate School of Education, 1972).
7. Peter Scharf and Joseph Hickey, *Towards a Just Community in Prison* (San Francisco: Jossey-Bass, 1979).
8. Joseph Reimer, "Moral Reasoning among Israeli Kibbutz Adolescents" (unpublished thesis, Harvard Graduate School of Education, 1977).
9. Robert L. Selman and Dan Jaquette, "To Understand and To Help: Implications of Developmental Research for the Education of Children with Interpersonal Problems," in *Readings in Moral Education,* ed. Peter Scharf (Minneapolis, Minn.: Winston Press, 1978).
10. Harry Stack Sullivan, *The Interpersonal Theory of Psychiatry* (New York: Norton, 1953).

# Chapter II
## Dilemmas as Tools
## for Developmental Moral Education

# Reasons for Using Moral Dilemmas
# in the Classroom

To accept the cognitive developmental approach to moral education is first to accept the empirical psychological findings that as humans mature they acquire and develop a sense of justice and second to agree philosophically that this is the way it should be. If these two ideas are accepted, it's easy to define the goal of moral education as twofold: to stimulate the healthy development (to higher stages) of children's moral reasoning and to stimulate children to act according to their increased moral judgment. Given the goal, it's natural for the teacher to ask: How is development stimulated? What can I do to aid the development of moral reasoning in my students?

Researchers in developmental moral education have found the moral dilemma and its accompanying discussion to be the most useful curriculum tools in classroom developmental moral education. Kohlberg suggests that the experience of moral conflict and the awareness of the perspectives and opinions of others are directly related to full and rapid moral growth. The moral dilemma serves as a means of focusing on moral conflict through a specific situation. As students in a group respond to a dilemma, they naturally offer different concepts of what they believe to be right and wrong. The sharing of diverse moral opinions forces students in the group to either clarify and reiterate their own moral stances or to integrate the opinions of others into their own moral beliefs. This sharing of moral reasoning also forces each of the participants to experience conflict, or disequilibrium, as he or she finds his or her ideas challenged by the ideas and viewpoints of others.

This atmosphere of conflict is an ideal environment for moral growth, for the more a child is exposed to thinking at a stage higher than his or her own, the more likely the child will be to move to that stage.

# The Moral Dilemma Defined

Basically, a moral dilemma is a conflict situation in which what's right or wrong isn't clearcut or obvious. Examples of moral dilemmas might raise questions like whether or not it's ever right to steal, or to lie, or to take a human life. Questions like these raise uncomfortable issues and feelings about moral responsibilities, customs, habits, and obligations. They make one stop and think.

A good, workable dilemma involves a specific situation, isn't cluttered with too much information, and is both interesting *and* plausible to the individuals who are expected to respond to it. Successful dilemmas—those which serve to nudge children to higher stages of moral growth—have certain qualities in common, though their form and content may differ radically (as will be obvious in the workbook section of this text). Here are some characteristics of effective dilemmas:

- Effective dilemmas present conflicting claims, both or all of which *on the surface* appear to be reasonable. For example, a dilemma dealing with a conflict between human life and law is powerful because most people believe in both the importance of life and in the individual's responsiblity to the law. Similarly, a dilemma involving a conflict between telling the truth and hurting someone's feelings is powerful because most people prefer neither to lie nor to hurt someone else.
- Effective dilemmas focus at a particular transitional stage level. For example, a good dilemma for children at Stages 2 and 3 might focus on issues of concern for others versus an individual's self-interest. (Should you stop to help a friend who's had a bike accident if you're late getting home for your birthday party?)  Similarly, a good dilemma for students at Stages 3 and 4 might involve a conflict between the law and group allegiance. (Should you turn in a good friend who you know has committed a crime?)
- Effective dilemmas involve some life experience that's real to the participants' own situations. For example, most dilemmas which evoke response from elementary school children involve problems with peers or parents. (Should you lie to your parents in order to go to a movie with your friends?)
- Effective dilemmas often use historical or scientific cases, but the facts are clearly defined and limited so that the primary focus is on the *ethical* issue rather than on the practical or scientific or historical ones.
- Effective dilemmas open the way for discussion questions which force children to think more deeply about the moral issues contained within the dilemmas. For example, a teacher

using a dilemma dealing with animal experimentation (Should scientists be allowed to inject animals with dangerous drugs in order to find a cure for a serious disease?) might raise the following questions:

a) What is the moral problem here?
b) Do you think scientists should be able to use animals this way?
c) What rights do the sick people have who might be cured by the discoveries?
d) What's the difference between using people for experiments and using animals for experiments?

## Dilemma and Discussion

As the preceding example indicates, perhaps the most common use of the moral dilemma is to stimulate Socratic open-ended *discussion.* Through a free sharing of opinions about a dilemma and through the Socratic probing and challenging of student opinions by the teacher, children are placed in cognitive disequilibrium, or conflict, and gradually move toward more mature moral philosophies.

A successful dilemma discussion usually involves the following series of steps:

- First, the teacher attempts to clarify any ambiguous facts in the moral dilemma.
- Second, the teacher encourages a broad reaction to the dilemma by asking an open-ended question (for example, *What's the problem here?* or, *What's the right thing to do?).*
- Third, the teacher helps the class understand positions taken by individual students or characters in the dilemma or poses positions which might realistically be taken. At this point, the discussion ceases to be directed at the dilemma itself and becomes instead a process in which students challenge one another's *reasoning* about the dilemma.
- Finally, through probes and analogies, the teacher attempts to place particular opinions in conflict and thus move the group to a greater understanding of the dilemma and the moral concepts it contains.

Teachers clearly play a critical role in the dilemma discussion process: they're responsible for presenting and sometimes recognizing or even creating provocative and educationally stimulating dilemma situations; they must always maintain a trusting, supportive, yet *controlled* classroom climate in which a democratic discussion can take place; they must be willing to participate with the students in a process of mutual moral education and growth.

*The primary role of the teacher,* however, is to stimulate conflict among students and then to guide those students toward resolution of the conflict. This process is essential to cognitive reorganization and therefore to moral growth. The moral dilemma is an effective tool in this process. Let's look at a sample dilemma and examine ways in which it might be used by a teacher with his or her class.

Dresel Sports Equipment, Inc., is located in a small town. It's been making basketballs for many years and hires about two hundred workers who live in the town. During its operation, the company dumps dangerous chemicals and waste matter into the river which runs through the town. The river has become so polluted that the state government agency which works to protect the environment has sent an inspector, Ms. Smith, to look into the situation.

Ms. Smith has found that many fish are dying because of the pollution and that the water going to towns down the river has also become polluted. She's asked the company to stop polluting the river, but the owners are arguing that they can't because it would be too expensive to get rid of the wastes in any other way. They say that they'd have to go out of business if they had to follow the government antipollution requirements. A lot of workers would lose their jobs. The company also says that they can't even partly clean up the river unless they lay off ten to twenty workers to help pay for the cost of the cleanup.

In any situation like this, each conflicting element has some moral validity. Clean, healthy air, water, and land are valued—but so are jobs. Manufactured products are valued. Laws are involved. Possible consequences must be considered. The clashing moral claims named here make this situation a moral dilemma.

The issues contained in this dilemma may be confronted in at least four ways: through study, thought, discussion, and action. Obviously, none of these is completely distinct from the others. Studying the dilemma might require learning about the scientific concepts involved; for example, what things are good for living creatures and what things aren't? It also might necessitate taking a look at existing laws. Which are reasonable and which aren't? Economic factors are important, too. Could the company raise the price of their basketballs to pay the costs of pollution control without losing business to competitors? If the company decided to clean up the river, could the workers who were laid off get jobs elsewhere?

Once students start thinking about these issues, an atmosphere of conflict is created. Discussing the dilemma and its elements is one way of getting the students to think about what the dilemma really means. Anyone who actively participates in a discussion is forced to think about the issues involved. In addition, discussion allows the teacher and students to share their thoughts. Writing about pollution, role-playing possible confrontations between company representatives and Ms. Smith or between company representatives and the workers, and doing related art projects are other ways of approaching the dilemma. Carrying the dilemma further—by, for example, talking about pollution in the students' own town—can result in the students' taking action themselves by writing letters to industry or government figures, organizing cleanup activities, or trying to influence other people.

Developmental educators usually consider discussion the best way of getting at the issues present in a moral dilemma. But discussion is more than a vehicle for thought; it requires active participation in a social setting. Discussion forces participants to deal with people and issues at the same time. It's especially important, then, for the teacher to establish an atmosphere of freedom of expression and mutual acceptance of other people and their ideas. In an atmosphere like this, children will be willing to participate. Most people enjoy discussing moral conflicts, and most children will do so eagerly if they know ahead of time that their contributions will be accepted. Ideally, teachers will direct the flow of the discussion while allowing the students to do most of the talking.

# Matching Dilemmas to Students' Level of Development

Having seen that dilemma discussions can be used to both stimulate conflict in a classroom and bring about conflict resolution, or growth, we need to examine what kinds of dilemmas can work best under what circumstances. Since each class is different, and each child within a class is a unique individual, there's no cut-and-dried way of approaching this problem. That is, rural children may not understand matters that inner-city children will grasp quite readily, and vice-versa; nor will an eleven-year-old child be able to comprehend a dilemma involving purely adult concerns. Basically, an effective dilemma contains both situations and issues which are familiar and plausible to the students. The concept of *developmental match* can help us to understand what kinds of dilemmas can be most useful and why some are more useful than others.

While children are able to understand reasoning at or below the stage they themselves are in, and sometimes one stage above, they're almost never able to comprehend arguments *more than one stage* above them. Thus, the teachers must attempt to match dilemmas to the developmental stages of their students and introduce conflict by posing questions at the next higher stages.

This isn't as difficult as it may seem. Most teachers have a pretty good idea of where the students in their class are in their moral development merely by observing them and interacting with them all day, every day. The concerns of most upper elementary school children are similar. They worry about how other people see them; they're concerned about their relationships with their parents and peers. They want others to like them. Many don't spend a lot of time thinking about what's going on in the adult world except as it directly affects them or the people they care about.

A working knowledge of Kohlberg's theory can help us find dilemmas that will be interesting to children while at the same time providing sufficient conflict to move them to higher stages. Other than that, the process of developmental match rests largely—at least at first—on trial and error. A dilemma that's too far above students' heads might not do them any good, but it probably won't do them any harm, either, and it's easy enough to discard it and move on to a better one.

Even though the process of discovering which dilemmas work and why may be initially frustrating, it helps us to learn more about our students and how they think. When a dilemma "misses" the student audience, it forces us to confront the fact that they think differently than we do—and we learn something, too.

# Techniques for Conducting Dilemma Discussions

In 1967, Moshe Blatt conducted two very successful classroom moral development programs. The methods he developed still serve as good examples of techniques we might use in our own classrooms.

The teachers using the Blatt method followed a strategy which sought to stimulate moral conflict through guided moral discussion. A typical class discussion session in one of these programs usually ran as follows.

The teacher first presented a dilemma story to the class. (The dilemmas used were similar to the ones found in the Workbook section of this text.) After the class had had a chance to discuss the dilemma briefly, the teacher asked them to think about possible solutions to the dilemma. He recorded these solutions on a chalkboard for all to see. Then he asked the students to consider the consequences of each solution. At this point, the class attempted to think through and verbalize the underlying moral values, rules, standards, or principles inherent in each solution. They tried to think of the *generalizations* for which the solutions were *specific* examples. These generalizations, or standards, became the real topics of the discussion. Again, it's important to keep in mind that a dilemma is only a tool; the teacher's objective in a moral discussion should be to help the students look at the reasons they have for a particular solution to a problem.

The differences in moral reasoning among the students resulted in spontaneous arguments about the worthiness or adequacy of the moral standards or generalizations and how they could be applied to the dilemma under discussion. The teacher tried to stimulate controversy in these arguments by introducing questions and issues which resulted in further conflict among the students. As the arguments developed, he took a solution proposed by a student who was arguing at one stage *above* the majority of the class and clarified and supported that student's position. He elaborated on the solution and its generalizations—and the reasoning the student used to arrive at that solution—until he felt that the majority of the students understood its logic and seemed convinced that its logic was at least reasonable or fair.

However, the teacher attempted to leave as much of the argument as possible to the students themselves. He stepped in only when it was necessary to summarize the discussion or to clarify a point. Students who argued at higher levels were encouraged to point out why the lower stage arguments were incomplete or inadequate. When the teacher felt that the higher stage students were unable to point out the weaknesses of the lower stage arguments, he attempted to rephrase the higher stage argument so that the rest of the class could understand it.

The important features of Blatt's method are first, his attempt to confront students with the inadequacies and inconsistencies of their lower stage reasoning; second, his insistence on focusing on reasoning rather than the dilemma itself; and third, his awareness of developmental match. It's also significant to note that throughout all of the discussions, the teacher tried to establish and maintain an atmosphere in which freedom of expression was protected and in which understanding of alternative views was encouraged.

We can use Blatt's program to arrive at some useful guidelines for conducting moral discussions:

1. *Clarify the facts within a dilemma.*
   - Make sure that all students understand the dilemma. If using a fictional or historical dilemma, such as those in the Workbook section of this book, read it aloud yourself or have one student read it aloud to the others. Give the children a chance to read it over to themselves if they want to. List important facts, events, or names on the chalkboard for reference.
   - Don't initiate a discussion on an ambiguous or confusing dilemma. If the children don't seem to understand the issues contained in a certain dilemma, go on to another

one. Make sure the dilemma is clear to you before opening it up for discussion.

2. *Clarify the issues involved.*
   - Focus on genuine moral conflicts. While these may either be real issues drawn from the students' lives and the world around them or hypothetical dilemmas, they should always be provocative and interesting to the children.
   - Try to distinguish among the moral and the strategic, or practical, issues within a dilemma. For example, differentiate between what a person *would* do in a particular situation and what he or she *should* do. Focus on what a person *should* do.
   - Give children enough time to build coherent arguments and take firm positions about specific issues within a dilemma.

3. *Create an atmosphere of trust in the classroom.*
   - Initially, support almost any idea clearly related to the problem at hand.
   - Try to create a climate in which students are encouraged to understand one another's positions. Point out differences among their arguments while making it obvious that you respect each person's point of view. Be willing to offer your opinions, while making it clear that you consider the children's opinions as important and valid as your own.
   - Try to establish a sense of fairness and justice within the group as a whole.
   - Encourage broad participation among students of both sexes, differing physical statures, and diverse social positions within the class. Avoid letting one student or a group of relatively few students dominate the discussion.
   - Don't let students interrupt another who's speaking until that person has had a chance to build a coherent argument.
   - Encourage questions which challenge the children's intellectual and moral reasoning, but never their integrity or worth. Try to instill each individual with a sense of his or her own worth.
   - Keep the discussion controlled enough that children can hear one another. While encouraging diverse viewpoints, keep children from harshly criticizing one another's viewpoints. Don't let a discussion become so fragmented that its point is lost.
   - Avoid making arbitrary or unfair procedural decisions.

4. *Encourage the children to develop and grow.*
   - Try to encourage democratic dialogue among children at adjacent stages. Developmental theory holds that a Stage 2 child will experience greater conflict from a Stage 3 argument than from either a Stage 4 or a Stage 1 argument.
   - Don't argue several stages above (or below ) the students in your group nor present them with dilemmas they can't understand or aren't interested in.
   - Help students become aware of the reasoning processes they use to arrive at solutions to a dilemma.
   - Watch for inconsistencies and inadequacies in the arguments used. Highlight contradictions.
   - If possible, find ways of resolving the inconsistencies and inadequacies in the children's arguments. Make clear, however, that not everyone has to agree on one solution or one approach to a dilemma.

# Beyond Discussion: Moral Dilemmas and School Life

Moral education shouldn't stop when a dilemma discussion does. Ideally, it's an ongoing process, and one that should be emphasized throughout the school day. One way in which a teacher can become more involved in his or her students' moral education is by applying the skills learned in dilemma discussion to the resolution of real-life conflicts. For example, a teacher might ask the students to decide whether they should have the right to chew gum in class rather than deciding for them. Or, he or she might involve the class in a democratic discussion about what kinds of punishments are fair for students who break class rules. This doesn't mean, of course, that children should be allowed to do whatever they please. Again, the teacher should take the role of guiding the discussion so that the children come to better—and better understood—conclusions than they would if left to themselves.

In one California elementary school, where fighting on the playground was causing problems, a teacher used the following dilemma to start the students thinking about the moral issues involved in fighting—and in stopping fights.

Chad and two of his friends, Mary and Phil, were spending Saturday afternoon playing Frisbee in the park when they noticed two younger boys fighting. They looked like they were really going at it, too, and were making a lot of noise.

"Let's break up that fight," Phil suggested. "There must be a better way for them to settle their problems."

"No, wait," Chad said. "I think we should stay out of it. It's none of our business."

One of the younger boys finally got the better of the other and started kicking him. Mary sided with Phil. "Come on, let's break it up," she said. "Someone might get hurt if we don't."

"I still think we ought to mind our own business," Chad answered. "Nobody's going to get hurt. They're both too little to hurt each other. Let's go somewhere else and play."

He managed to convince Phil and Mary, and the three of them walked off to another part of the park.

After clarifying the dilemma with the children and allowing time for questions, the teacher began the discussion.

**Teacher:** Was Chad right? Did he and his two friends do the right thing by not stopping the fight?
**Chorus:** NO!
**Teacher:** Why not?
**Cynara:** The little kids could hurt themselves. They really should talk it over and not fight.
**Heidi:** But if Chad and his friends stopped the fight, they might have gotten hurt, too.
**Teacher:** But the fighters were only two little boys. They couldn't have hurt the three older kids.
**Caren:** I think that Chad was right and the other two were right, too. Chad was right because the little kids could have just been play-fighting. The other two were right because the fighters might have gotten hurt.
**Kim:** If the older kids had broken it up, the little kids might have just started fighting again anyway when the older kids left.
**Linda:** There's a saying that if someone is fighting you should just mind your own business. But the people who are fighting could get hurt. Both of them are right.
**Teacher:** In some situations it might be better to mind your own business and in other situations it might be best to interfere. Which is right here? Why?

**Caren:** I'd probably break them up . . . because they could get hurt.

**Shelly:** Well, they could be fighting and maybe be rolling around and maybe roll off a curb and be hurt by a car. Then it'd be in the papers, and if the older kids read about it they might think, "Wow, if I'd stopped the fight then the little kids might not have been hurt."

**Kim:** It'd be on their conscience.

**Teacher:** What about Chad's argument? When he says that they should mind their own business, he means that the little kids have a right to fight if they want to.

**Shelly:** Well, if someone comes up and hits you in the mouth, then you might want to hit them back. Sometimes you don't want to fight but somebody makes you.

**Teacher:** Is minding your own business a good rule to follow most of the time?

**Ron:** It depends.

**Linda:** Like when two people are having a private conversation.

**Cynara:** One time I got really mad at someone because I was having an argument with someone else and this person butted right in.

**Teacher:** If minding your own business is usually a good rule to follow, what's different about this situation?

**Kim:** What's different is that someone might get hurt.

**Cynara:** Like, if someone's an alcoholic, then maybe you shouldn't mind your own business because it's better to help them.

**Teacher:** What is it that makes you feel like you should keep somebody from getting hurt? Why should you bother to help somebody?

**Shelly:** You feel sorry for them. It's like, if you were them, then you'd know how they felt. I mean, if it was you, you'd want people to help you, so why shouldn't you help other people?

In discussing this dilemma, the teacher tried to get the students to suggest a rule about when (and whether) it might be right for one person to get involved in another person's problem. The teacher tried to get the group to understand that the younger boys in the dilemma situation might get hurt and that the older children have an obligation to intervene under these circumstances. Developmental theory suggests that this type of discussion will, in the long run, have a positive influence on school discipline problems as children come to understand their obligations to others in a more mature fashion. This understanding forms the basis for an orderly, as well as open and democratic, school environment.

## Deciding When and Where to Use Moral Dilemmas

Because moral dilemmas are so definitely a part of everyday life (think back on Sandy Curtis), they don't necessarily have to be scheduled into precise niches of a curriculum. Most children find dilemmas fun to listen to, read, and talk about, and welcome them at almost any time. Moral dilemma discussions can, however, serve very definite purposes in specific times and places; use the following as guidelines.

1. *Moral dilemma discussions can be used for guidance and affective education.*

    The simplest and most obvious context for moral education is the time allocated for guidance, affective education, civics, ethics, current events, or similar activities. During any of these times, feel free to use the dilemma discussion as an end in itself—an experience designed to stimulate reflective moral thinking. Introduce dilemmas as "interesting stories" or "something you might like to think about." Dilemmas involving relationships with peers or parents might be especially appropriate at times like these.

2. *Classroom matters, rules, and discipline can be seen as opportunities for moral dilemma discussions.*

    Situations which require disciplinary action often provide opportunities for teachers and students alike to examine social rules and relationships. Moral dilemmas which deal with rules or conflicting relationships with peers might be used by teachers who are concerned about social or behavioral problems they see in their students. For example, the dilemma "Eddie and the Lunch Line" (see page 78) was effectively used by a teacher whose class had been identified as "cut-takers" by the lunchline monitors.

    If a disciplinary problem has occurred often enough to make it troublesome, pose the problem as a dilemma and then discuss possible solutions. Depending on the situation, you may permit students to single out behaviors which disrupt the class. Note, however, that the exact moment at which a behavioral problem is occurring is not the best time to begin a moral discussion about it. It's better to discuss the problem (or similar dilemma) at another time, perhaps between occurrences of the problem if the problem is frequent or after an outburst has settled down.

Keep in mind that moral dilemma discussions won't in and of themselves solve behavior problems; nor are they meant to replace effective disciplinary methods. Dilemma discussions can, however, provide opportunities for educationally meaningful dialogues about conflicting rights and responsibilities, the effects of which can carry over into the students' lives outside the classroom.

Other classroom matters, such as the need to establish rules and procedures, can afford excellent opportunities for moral education. Discussions of fairness, for example, are often natural and spontaneous. If there are thirty children in a class and only two recess balls, you might want to use that situation as a basis for discussing fair and right ways of sharing the balls over time.

Many aspects of classroom life can be used to advantage for moral education purposes. If you involve the students in some of these decisions, you give them a greater chance to grow than you would if you simply laid down rules for them to follow—no matter how fair your rules might be. The effects of this approach will be obvious as the children develop a more positive attitude toward you, the class, and one another.

3. *Moral education can be integrated into academic subjects.*

Certain subjects, like history, social studies, science, and reading, abound in moral dilemmas. Making use of them provides more than just extra chances for discussion sessions—it also helps to draw the students deeper into the subject matter. First, it encourages them to get the facts necessary for a worthwhile discussion. Second, dilemma discussions tend to draw students into the issues and help them to clarify them in their own minds. In other words, discussion ensures careful thought about the subject matter.

4. *And, finally, moral dilemma discussions can occur spontaneously.*

Although moral problems concern most of us a good part of the time, they're often overlooked because they're not recognized as such. Many issues which have moral dimensions occur in academic subjects, current events, school affairs, and our private lives. These dilemmas provide excellent opportunities for making use of developmental moral education, as well as for conducting real and relevant discussions. When issues surface in the classroom, take time to discuss their moral aspects.

# Chapter III

# Using Moral Discussions:
Three Dilemmas

# The Moral Discussion Process: "The Spelling Test"

Most teachers find that conducting dilemma discussions with elementary school children can be educationally profitable and rewarding, particularly if such discussions follow a fairly specific order of *phases,* or steps. These phases were mentioned briefly in Chapter Two. We will list them again and then examine them more carefully.

- First, the children and the teacher work together to clarify the elements of the dilemma.
- Second, the teacher elicits the children's initial responses to the dilemma and encourages those who are reluctant to participate to do so.
- Third, the group as a whole explores and tries to comprehend the different positions and opinions voiced by individual group members.
- And finally, the teacher probes the children's opinions and perhaps amplifies or extends the dilemma via analogy or comparison.

To illustrate this process, let's look at the highlights of a dilemma discussion that took place among a group of fourth graders in a California public school. We'll attempt to describe the discussion itself while at the same time illustrating the four phases mentioned above.

The complete discussion lasted for about a half hour. (Some repetitive parts have been deleted.) Most of the students in the group seemed genuinely involved and interested.

The teacher began the session by passing out copies of the dilemma to each student. After giving the children a chance to look over the dilemma, she read it aloud to them. Here is the dilemma.

## The Spelling Test

Every Wednesday morning, the teacher gave the sixth-grade class a spelling test—twenty-five words from their weekly lessons, and five hard bonus words. The highest scorer in the class was rewarded with an extra free period during the afternoon. Whenever April won the free period, she spent time in the art room. She was working on a special gift for her mother's birthday.

April and two of her friends, Mary and Lisa, sat close together in class. During this Wednesday's spelling test, April saw Mary slip a small piece of paper to Lisa. The paper had the five bonus words written on it. Mary had prepared it before the test.

When the scores were added up, April realized what her friends' cheating would mean. Lisa was the only person in the class to get all thirty words right. April had missed only one, a bonus word, and had the next best score. Mary had missed three of the regular words.

April had a decision to make. She felt that cheating was wrong—and besides, if she told on Mary and Lisa, she'd get the free period. At the same time, she didn't *want* to get her friends in trouble.

After reading the dilemma aloud, the teacher began the discussion by introducing the goals she had for the session as well as outlining some general guidelines.

**Teacher:**  Before we start talking about the story, I want to remind you that we should all let other people say what they want to say without interrupting them. We should all try to accept what people in the class say without making fun of them or their opinions or feelings. It's really important to remember this. If we want to have a good discussion, then we have to make sure that everyone has a chance to participate. People aren't going to want to participate if they don't think that we'll accept the things they say. You don't have to agree with someone else's opinions—you can disagree with them and still accept what they have to say. So let's all try to be polite to each other and be good listeners.

Now I've read the story to you about April and her friends and the spelling test. Does everyone understand what's going on in the story?
**All:**  Yes.
**Teacher:**  Can someone summarize the problem?
**Student:**  April isn't sure whether or not she should report Lisa and Mary for cheating.

In other dilemmas, of course—such as those which have complex historical settings—the teacher may have to explain the facts and make sure that the students understand what happens in the story itself. In this case, the first phase of the dilemma discussion—that of clarifying the elements of the dilemma—was taken care of quickly and easily.

The teacher entered the second phase of the dilemma discussion by beginning with a very general question, designed to elicit broad student participation.

**Teacher:** What do you think is the right thing for April to do? Should she tell on her friends, or shouldn't she?

Several students immediately responded with some fairly short statements of their opinions:

**Kathie:** She should tell.
**Teacher:** Why?
**Kathie:** Because it isn't right to cheat. Lisa got a good score just because she cheated.
**Teacher:** John, do you have a different opinion?
**John:** I think Lisa should get busted because she cheated.
**Devon:** I think April should tell because she . . . well . . . I don't know.
**Teacher:** How about you, Susan?
**Susan:** I think April should tell because she deserves the free period and Lisa doesn't. Why should Lisa get rewarded for cheating?
**Steven:** Lisa shouldn't get the free period because she cheated. And maybe another time when she takes a test or something she'll get a lot wrong.

At this point in the discussion, there seemed to be a general consensus that April should tell on her friends for cheating. Then the teacher tried to find out if there was anybody in the class who disagreed, who believed that April should *not* tell. Other children who believed that she shouldn't may have been too shy to speak their minds. In order to have full participation, the teacher knew it was necessary for these children to feel that they could speak out.

**Teacher:** Is there anybody who feels that April shouldn't tell?
**Jeff:** Well, kinda. . .
**Teacher:** Why, Jeff?
**Jeff:** Because they're her friends—Lisa and Mary are April's friends.
**Maggie:** Yeah, and if she told on them, they might get mad and not like her anymore.

**Teacher:** Do you agree with that, Jeff?

**Jeff:** Not exactly. I just think you shouldn't get your friends in trouble.

Beginning the third phase, the teacher reiterates the arguments for and against April's telling on her friends. She tries to help the students understand one another's positions.

**Teacher:** Okay. Some of you disagree on whether or not April should tell. Susan feels that Lisa should not be rewarded for cheating, so April *should* tell. Maggie thinks April's friends won't like her if she tells. And Jeff feels that you shouldn't get your friends into trouble. Let's look at these opinions more closely. Do you think April will lose her friends if she tells?

**Susan:** What kind of friends are they if they know April deserved the free period and they got it instead? It's not fair.

**Steven:** They might be mad for a while but then I think they'd see that getting the free period by cheating wasn't fair to the kids who didn't cheat.

**Teacher:** What about Jeff's idea that you shouldn't tell on your friends?

**Steven:** If April tells, then the teacher can help the girls who cheated. That's what teachers are paid for. April should tell so the teacher can help Lisa and Mary.

Steven suggested a possible Stage 3 alternative, stating that April should tell because teachers are obligated to help and teach people. If no one tells on cheaters, then teachers won't be able to help students as much as they should be able to. Steven's reasoning was a step in the right direction, but the teacher realized that before the rest of the class could accept his answer they'd have to fully understand Susan's Stage 2 argument, so she probed further:

**Teacher:** Does it make a difference here whether there's a free period prize or not?

**Jeff:** Yes. If they didn't have a free period, I wouldn't tell. If they did have one, I would tell.

**Devon:** That's wrong. I wouldn't tell just to get the free period. I would tell because it's for their own good.

The teacher attempted to force the question about which reason for telling was the *best* reason, and tried to move the class to conflict so they'd think through a more mature—or Stage 3—answer to the dilemma.

**Teacher:** Okay, some people say you should tell so you can get the free period. Other people say that you should tell so that you can help the people who cheat. Which is the best reason for telling? Which is the most right?

Devon and Maggie responded with what appear to be at least partially Stage 3 arguments:

**Devon:** Telling to help the person is a better reason because then you aren't just thinking about yourself. If you tell just because you want the free period, then you're being selfish. If you tell for the other reason, then you're thinking about other people, too, and what's good for them.

**Maggie:** Yeah, telling for the reward is just for fun. If you tell for the other reason, you're learning something.

This discussion was typical in many ways of the kinds of dilemma discussions we can expect to have with upper elementary school children. The students were very much involved in the discussion process and offered a range of Stage 1, 2, and 3 moral opinions. The teacher helped the students look at the *reasons* for taking particular moral positions rather than simply accepting what she might have believed to be the right opinion. By the end of the discussion, we can see that the children were at least considering a Stage 3 reason as the best one. Their Stage 1 or 2 arguments had been faced with a more adequate Stage 3 argument which was sufficiently explored to start them thinking about its validity.

# Recognizing Stages: "Eddie and the Lunch Line"

In order for a teacher to effectively lead a moral dilemma discussion, he or she must be able to recognize, at least in a general way, the moral stages of the arguments which children use. Detecting the differences in the stage responses is a skill which the good teacher or discussion leader needs to cultivate. Keep in mind, however, that a child may offer responses which reflect more than one stage.

Let's look at another typical discussion, this time involving fifth grade students, to see whether it's possible to recognize the particular moral stages used in their arguments. The dilemma was enthusiastically received by the children, and they were eager to begin discussing it.

Again, the teacher began by passing out copies of the dilemma, giving the children a chance to look it over, and then reading it aloud.

## Eddie and the Lunch Line

Eddie felt lucky. He had P.E. just before noon, and the gym was right next to the cafeteria, so if he hurried he could be among the first kids in line at the cafeteria door. It was the last day before summer vacation, and the school always served a special lunch on that day—hamburgers and ice-cream bars. Ice-cream bars were Eddie's favorite food. On days like this, the line got long fast.

Eddie managed to get near the head of the line. Eddie's friend Tom had to come all the way from a class at the other end of the building. There were over sixty kids waiting by the time Tom arrived.

Tom walked up to Eddie and said, "Let me in front of you, man. I'll give you my ice cream."

The discussion proceeded as follows:

**Teacher:** Should Eddie let Tom in line?

**Sam:** No.

**Mark:** It wouldn't be fair to the other kids. The other kids would have to wait one person longer. If everyone did that, it would take twice as long. The last guy might not get a whole lunch.

**Teacher:** What would be the right thing to do? Should Eddie tell him to go to the end of the line like everybody else?

**Mark:** There's other people in line. They have to wait too.

**Teacher:** Does it make a difference how many kids are in line?

**Liz:** Yes, it does. Sometimes the last people in line don't get a whole lunch.

**Sam:** No, it doesn't, because if everyone took cuts and the last people didn't let their friends take cuts, it would still be unfair.

**Teacher:** What would the kids behind Eddie think if he let Tom in line?

**Liz:** They would think that he's a mean brat. That he wasn't a friend.

**Sam:** He shouldn't let him in. He should tell him to go to the back. He should know that the kids in line won't think it's fair. If he was further back in line and someone ahead of him let his friend cut in, he wouldn't like it.

**Teacher:** How do you think Tom is going to feel if Eddie says no? Do you think that he'll think Eddie isn't a good friend?

**Liz:** In a way, but he'll probably think later on that taking cuts isn't fair for the other kids. Anyway, if you do something like that, you lose a lot of friends, not just one.

**Teacher:** So what's wrong about taking cuts?

**Sam:** It's not fair to the other kids.

**Tracy:** Yeah, if Tom's at the end of the line, maybe it's because he played around getting there. So Tom shouldn't have an unfair advantage.

**Teacher:** Is there any time when it's okay to take cuts?

**Colleen:** When there are only two people in line and the other person says it's okay.

**Barbara:** When you're at the end of the line, then you can let someone in front of you because nobody else will get mad.

**Tracy:** It would be okay if everyone behind Eddie said that they wouldn't mind if Tom took cuts. That wouldn't happen, though.

**Sam:** Maybe it'd be okay if the teacher gave him permission to cut in line because he had to hurry up with lunch and get back to do some work.

**Teacher:** Do you kids ever take cuts?

**All:** Yes!

Let's start by comparing Mark's, Sam's, and Liz's responses to the dilemma.

At first, Mark seems to have a higher stage concern for fairness and "other kids" in general. He begins by saying, "It wouldn't be fair to the other kids." He reveals his real concern, however, when he says, "The last guy might not get a complete lunch." This is a concrete Stage 2 argument; Tom's taking cuts will result in harm to another individual—that is, someone else might not get a complete lunch. A genuine Stage 3 argument, on the other hand, would take the whole group into account and not just one person.

Liz is aware of what others will think of Eddie—that "he's a mean brat . . . that he wasn't a friend." She also expresses concern that the other kids in line should be treated fairly. However, her major worry seems to be one of losing friends: "If you do something like that, you lose a lot of friends, not just one." Her argument is apparently a Stage 1 orientation toward consequences (losing friends), although she may also be struggling with a Stage 2 idea of reciprocal fairness.

Sam wavers between a sense of what's generally fair and a more personal stance: "He should know that the kids in line won't think it's fair. If he was further back in line and someone ahead of him let his friend cut in, he wouldn't like it." His second response—"It's not fair to the other kids"—seems to reveal a possible Stage 3 argument that the right thing to do is to take the perspective of the group as a whole. He feels that Eddie should be able to take the place of *anyone* in the line and understand how that person would feel.

This dilemma has been used in several discussion groups and has received many different responses. Some of them are given below, grouped according to stage level. By examining the differences in these arguments, we'll begin to more clearly see the patterns which indicate various stages. Note that responses for each stage include both pro and con positions. Keep in mind that the *solution to* a moral dilemma is less important to moral development than the *reasoning process* behind the solution.

1. *Stage 1 Responses to "Eddie and the Lunch Line":*
   *The Punishment and Obedience Orientation*
   - "Eddie should let him in. Then he'll get an extra ice cream. I'd take a free ice cream."
   - "No, he shouldn't, because he might not give it to him."
   - "No, he shouldn't, because he might get in trouble."
   - "No, 'cause he might get caught and then both of them would have to go to the end of the line."
   - "Tom's his friend. Tom would make him do it. If he didn't, then he might not play with him anymore or something."
2. *Stage 2 Responses to "Eddie and the Lunch LIne":*
   *The Instrumental-Relativist Orientation*
   - "Well, it's fair for Eddie because Tom will give him an ice cream." (Note the recognition of the element of fairness or reciprocity. The Stage 1 response emphasizes the getting of the ice cream rather than the exchange of favors.)
   - "If Eddie wants him to be in line with him, then it's okay."
   - "It's not fair to the other kids. If everyone took cuts, then it would take twice as long. It's not fair to the last person in line because they might run out of food."

- "If Eddie lets only Tom in, then it's all right for the other kids to tell the teacher. Eddie didn't let anyone else in. He only helped his friend. They don't owe him anything, like, not to tell."
- "It's okay if Tom has to eat lunch in a hurry."
- "People take cuts in front of us, so we can take cuts in front of them."
- "Tom's his friend. If he doesn't let him in, then Tom might not let Eddie in some other time. Tom wouldn't have to because Eddie didn't do it for him."

3. *Stage 3 Responses to "Eddie and the Lunch Line":*
   *The Interpersonal Concordance or "Good Boy/Good Girl"*
   *Orientation*
   - "It's not fair to the other kids. It's not the way a person is supposed to act in lines."
   - "Well, Tom's his friend. He should let him in. People always say you should stick by your friends."
   - "It's not fair to the other kids. If Eddie was back in line he wouldn't like it if someone else let another person in line. He should know how other people would feel."
   - "If Tom was a really good friend, he wouldn't try to bribe Eddie with the ice cream. Eddie should just let him in anyway. Because Tom's his really close friend."
   - "The teacher would say it's wrong."

4. *Stage 4 Responses to "Eddie and the Lunch Line":*
   *The Law and Order Orientation*
   - "No matter how you looked at it, Eddie would be breaking a rule if he let Tom in. He might have to explain to his friend that it's against the rules."
   - "It's not fair to the other kids. If everyone did that then that would be breaking the rules. For our school and other places like this to run well and fairly, we need to follow the rules."
   - "Tom's his friend, and he might *want* to let him in, but he shouldn't anyway. Someone shouldn't break a rule just to help a friend."

While recognizing stages may seem difficult at first, the more one works with moral dilemma discussions, the clearer the stages become. Experience clarifies differences that may not be apparent at the outset.

The key to distinguishing stages is avoiding surface rhetoric and looking for deeper thinking processes. For example, the above groups of Stage 1, 2, and 3 answers all contain one which begins, "Tom's his friend." If the teacher had stopped the students at this point, he or she might have been tempted to regard each of these answers as evidence of Stage 3 thinking because of its seeming orientation to friendship. By allowing the students to continue and elaborate on their responses, however, the teacher discovers several different levels of reasoning hidden behind the rhetoric of friendship.

The Stage 1 responses show an awareness of and respect for power ("Tom would make him do it.") and/or physical consequences, both good and bad. ("He might not play with him anymore," "He might get caught," and "He might get in trouble.") Note the differences between the Stage 1 orientation toward *consequences* and the Stage 2 consciousness of *reciprocity,* or the exchange of favors. Consequences come only from without, perhaps from the other person. Reciprocity is a two-way street where both the self and the other are necessary to effect the exchange, and where the self is aware of the moral claims of both the self and the other. The Stage 2 child sees this reciprocity as "fairness."

Another point at which the stage responses might seem confusing concerns the Stage 1 concept of consequences and the Stage 2 concept of *need satisfaction* (or *instrumentalism*). Where the Stage 1 child may see something as "right" because it brings about favorable consequences, the Stage 2 child looks for something which he or she desires or needs and is willing to exchange something for it. In the examples above, we see how the Stage 1 response that it's right to let Tom in line simply *because* this means that Eddie will get an extra ice cream contrasts with the Stage 2 concept of exchange. The Stage 2 child is apt to believe that Eddie may let Tom in line because he's exchanging this favor in order to fulfill his desire for more ice cream. It's no longer a question of the ice cream being a *reward;* instead, it's become an *exchange* situation involving the satisfaction of a need or desire. Other examples of Stage 2 instrumental need satisfaction are, "If Eddie wants him to be in line with him, then it's okay," or, "It's okay if Tom has to eat lunch in a hurry." However, we should be aware of the brevity of these responses and the possibility that further questioning might have revealed reasoning at different stages.

It should be pointed out that Stage 2 exchange may involve animosity as well as favors. Examples of such negative exchanges are, "If Eddie lets him in, then it's all right for the other kids to tell the teacher," and, "People take cuts in front of us, so we can take cuts in front of them."

Looking at the Stage 3 responses which recognize that Tom is a friend, we see a consciousness of what we'll call the *third person*—the one (or ones) *outside* the immediate relationship between Eddie and Tom. The third person is the one who "always says you should stick by your friends." Here, the speakers have transcended the Stage 2 concept of simple exchange betweeen two parties by recognizing that the self and the other are both under the scrutiny of yet someone else (peers, parents, the teacher, society in general). This orientation to the third party ("what *they* will think about *me*") is the reason why Stage 3 is called the "good boy/good girl" stage.

The consciousness of legal authority and the social order (the law, the church, organized society) in the Stage 4 responses for the first time places a greater emphasis on the school's rules than upon friendships.

Remember, short statements are difficult to confidently place at a particular stage. The teacher must be willing to probe the student by asking more than one question in order to get a good understanding of the stage of reasoning the student uses. Suppose that the teacher asks, "Should Eddie let Tom in line?" and a child responds, "Yes." Obviously, a probe is needed, and the first choice is clearly, "Why?" or, "Why do you say/think that?" Suppose, again, that the student now responds, "Because Tom's his friend." As shown above, this reason is not sufficient to provide a basis for a stage judgment. The teacher can't yet have a thorough understanding of how the student views the concept of friendship and its relationships to the dilemma. So the teacher must choose a new probe. "Why" could be tried again, but experience has shown us that students usually react quickly and negatively to this. Repeating a question carries with it an element of intimidation or disapproval; a little creativity goes a long way. The teacher will get more information if he or she asks something like, "Explain what you mean by that," or "Tell me more." The best probes are probably specific questions, such as "How is friendship involved in this?" or "What is it about Tom's being Eddie's friend that makes it right to take cuts?"

## Generating Conflict: "Teapot Lake"

Up to this point in our examination of discussion techniques, we've been trying to show how the teacher can gain an understanding of the reasoning levels children use. We now turn to the technique of providing *conflict* for the student. Remember that it's important to try to make the student aware of the inconsistencies and inadequacies in his or her reasoning or arguments. In order to do this well, we must construct alternative situations or come up with arguments that represent thinking one stage above the student's. The student won't be able to resolve this argument if he or she sticks to his or her original argument or reasoning stage. The student may be led to see that his or her argument isn't "adequate" to resolve the new situation.

Let's look back for a moment at "Eddie and the Lunch LIne." To the Stage 1 child who says, "Tom's his friend. Tom would make him do it," we can counter with, "What about the other kids in line? Is Eddie being fair to them? If you were back in line, wouldn't you want to get your lunch as soon as possible without other kids taking cuts?" Or, we might try saying, "If Eddie lets Tom in, then is it okay for other kids to let their friends in, too? What if everyone did it?"

To the Stage 2 response, "Tom's his friend. If he doesn't let him in, then Tom might not let Eddie in some other time," we could reply by bringing the other kids in line into the situation as a third party with, "What would the other kids think about Eddie and Tom? Would they think it was right?" Notice how the third party status of the other kids in this case differs from their direct relationships to Eddie in the Stage 2 probe, "Is Eddie being fair to them?" The Stage 3 response, "People always say you should stick by your friends," can be met with the combination Stage 3 and 4 probe, "Yes, but don't people also say that you should follow the rules?" or the Stage 4 oriented question, "What's more important? The rules we live by, or what other people tell us or think about us?"

Quick thinking on the part of the teacher is the most difficult discussion technique to master, and it's something of an art. Fortunately, it isn't the only method—and may not even be the most productive one—for providing conflict. There are others, and one that's easiest on the teacher involves simply letting students challenge and provide conflict for one another. This approach is especially effective if the group contains students operating at different stages, which is usually the case.

The following is an edited transcript of a discussion among a group of sixth graders about the dilemma, "Teapot Lake." It illustrates a "natural" moral conflict in that the students themselves, rather than the teacher, do most of the active probing.

# Teapot Lake

While vacationing at Teapot Lake, Erica, her brother Bill, and his friend John decided to spend a whole day exploring an island in the middle of the lake. Erica and Bill's father took them out in his boat in the morning and told them that he'd return for them before dinnertime.

Just before noon, Bill fell and cut his leg. It bled badly, and it was obvious to the children that they couldn't wait until their father returned to get help.

John spotted a boathouse down by the beach and ran to see if anyone was there. No one was. There was nothing inside the boathouse but a rowboat. When he came back and told Erica about what he'd found, Erica suggested that they take the boat and row Bill across the lake to their cottage. Then it would only take them about ten minutes to get help for Bill.

John said, "We can't do that. The boathouse is locked."

"We can break the window and open the door from the inside," Erica suggested.

"But that's against the law!" John exclaimed. "We could get into a lot of trouble if we did that!"

"There isn't time to argue," Erica said. Then she ran to the boathouse, broke the window, crawled inside, and opened the door. She pulled the rowboat down to the shore and waited for John to help Bill into it.

**Teacher:** Was what Erica did right or wrong?

**Eddie:** I think it was right because Bill was hurt bad, and they couldn't wait. They'd be taking more of a chance by waiting than by breaking in to take the boat and then helping him. I don't think you'd get in as much trouble in a case like this as you would if nobody was hurt and you just broke in anyway.

**Dru:** After all, Bill is a person. Why should you risk a person's life for just a couple of years in jail?

**Chad:** He's going to jail!

**Nancy:** They had to steal it. They had a good reason.

**Teacher:** Okay, what was the good reason?

**Tony:** He was bleeding a lot.

**Nancy:** Well, I'll tell you. Is a boathouse more important than a person?

**Tony:** If they'd have just let him bleed, he probably would have died of blood loss. They had to do something.

**Chad:** If they went to court, they'd probably let them off because they saved that kid. The judge would probably say, "Okay, you saved somebody's life. That's good."

**Misti:** I think it depends on who the person is. If someone gets hurt, and you don't really know the person very well. . . .

**Teacher:** That's a good point. Should you do it for just anybody?

**Dru:** Yes!

**Tony:** Misti, think about someone you don't like. Would you help that person?

**Misti:** I don't think they should have helped that person if they weren't related.

**Mary:** You mean if a person was bleeding on the ground and you didn't know him you wouldn't help him?

**Misti:** (answering Mary) Not if it means that I'd have to break the law.

**Chad:** Why is your friend's life more important than someone else's?

**Al:** Because you like him and he likes you.

**Tony:** If you were walking down the street and there was a bum on the ground who had his leg cut real bad, wouldn't you help him?

**Misti:** Yeah, if I didn't have to break a law.

**Al:** No, it's not like a real friend.

**Eric:** How about if he couldn't breathe and he was all dirty and there was spit coming out of his mouth and you had to give him mouth-to-mouth resuscitation?

**Eddie:** Why not? Wouldn't you?

**Chorus:** Ohhh! Gross!

**Chad:** Hey, one at a time! One at a time!

**Teacher:** What is it about a person's life that would make you feel like helping someone?

**Tony:** I don't like to watch people die. And I just feel that I have to help them.

**Chad:** You only have one life. Why waste it?

**Mary:** I guess . . . It's like you could understand how the other person feels.

**Teacher:** In other words, you're saying that because you can put yourself in the other person's place you feel that you would want them to help you, so you feel that you should help them.

**Eddie:** I think that if I saw a person just bleeding on the street or something that I'd be to blame if I just stood there and watched or walked away. I'd feel like I killed the person.

**Tony:** That's what I would feel like, too.

**Chad:** Yeah, your conscience would be saying, "Why didn't you help the guy?" And you'd be thinking, "I bet that guy would be alive now if it hadn't been for me."

In this discussion, the teacher confines his role to that of simply eliciting reasons from the students (" . . . what's your reason? Be specific . . .") and restating their responses ("That's a good question. Should you do it for just anybody?"). Most of the conflict generation comes from the students themselves instead of the teacher. As they question and probe one another, they raise doubts about initial positions and begin to question the adequacy of one another's reasoning. For example, the other students are shocked and surprised by Misti's statement, "I don't think they should have helped that person if they weren't related." Several students challenge her argument. Mary asks, "You mean if a person was bleeding on the ground and you didn't know him you wouldn't help him?" and Chad assumes the role of professional group leader with his question, "Why is your friend's life more important than someone else's?" No teacher could have picked a better probe.

# Getting Started

By now, you should have a pretty good idea of what the theory of developmental moral education is all about and also some feeling for the methods which can be used to conduct dilemma discussions. The following summary can help you as you begin to put the theory into practice.


1. Choose an uncomplicated dilemma. Dilemmas dealing with peers or parents might be best to use at first, rather than historical or topical dilemmas in which the details of the situation require more attention.
2. Prepare the group or class for the discussion. Insist that students remain open to others' opinions. Point out that accepting another person's opinion isn't the same as agreeing with it. Emphasize that ridicule has no place in the discussion. An accepting atmosphere will encourage all students to participate and learn.
3. Read the dilemma aloud or present it in some other way. Give students the opportunity to clarify facts and people involved in the dilemma story. Write names, dates, and places on the chalkboard, if necessary, for easy reference.
4. Ask an opening question which requires the students to make a specific decision on the moral rightness or wrongness of the action which has been taken or might be taken. Many dilemmas are stories with "endings," while others are open. If a character in a dilemma has taken a decisive action or made a moral choice, it gives us the opportunity to ask the direct question, "Was what he/she did right or wrong? Why?" The "why" question is, of course, the important one, and the one on which the discussion should concentrate. For open-ended dilemmas, you'll want to start by eliciting possible endings for it, and then follow each suggestion with a "why." Keep the discussion focused on *moral* solutions and their reasons rather than purely expedient or practical solutions.
5. Watch how the students react to the dilemma. If they take off with the discussion, let them sustain it themselves for a while. If discussion falters, perhaps because all the participants reach a consensus of sorts, then develop a probe question. Write down on the chalkboard all the reasons which are offered as support for the students' opinions. Direct the discussion to the *quality* of these reasons. Which is the best? Which is the most right or moral? Encourage students arguing at the highest stage to defend their points of view to the others.

6. When a strong consensus seems to develop around a particular reasoning, make a decision whether or not to continue the discussion. Keep in mind the probable stage levels of the responses in your class, but avoid labeling individual students. Once you label children, you stop listening to them, and you may miss something important. The concept of developmental match should be used as a tool, not as an excuse for expecting the children to respond in certain ways and pushing them to respond in those ways.

   When the group is supporting an argument at a lower stage than you have good reason to suspect they're capable of, try to pose a higher stage contradiction to that argument. But do this cautiously. Think of a situation for which their argument wouldn't work, or come up with a conflicting moral force which runs counter to that argument (your friend, your parent, the law). The object, of course, is to force the students to confront the inadequacy of their argument.

   When the argument has been pushed to its limits, or when either the group or you yourself are exhausted, bring the discussion to a close.

7. After a few discussion sessions, try other types of dilemmas or activities. Discuss dilemmas which are real to your school or community. You may think of dilemma stories which are more appropriate for your class than the ones found in this book—feel free to adapt or create dilemmas.

   As students become familiar with the discussion process, try breaking the class into small student-led groups (with from three to eight participants, for example). While this approach sacrifices teacher direction, it increases student participation. Make sure that group leaders and members all have copies of the dilemmas being discussed. Assign each leader the task of managing the group and writing down the consensus opinion for each question (or the conflicting opinions). At the end of each session, ask group leaders to report their results to the entire class.

   Regardless of the form the discussion takes, children will find the activity interesting and rewarding as long as they're involved with dilemmas which present true conflicts of moral claims. It won't matter if these dilemmas are real or fictional. As one sixth grader put it, "Stories like this help us learn about life."

The remainder of this book is a workbook of dilemmas. You are given permission to duplicate these dilemmas for use with your students.

When you have distributed copies of the dilemma you intend to work with, read the dilemma with the students. You may have to provide the class with additional background for some of the dilemmas, particularly those involving current events, science, or history.

The questions given after each dilemma are meant to *guide* your discussion. It is not necessary to adhere strictly to the order in which these questions are given. Let the discussion flow from the students and insert the discussion questions judiciously as you proceed.

# Chapter IV

# Moral Dilemmas:
# A Workbook

# Dilemmas with Friends and Peers

Problems faced by children living and playing together.

# Barbara's Promise

Barbara and Suzanne lived three houses away from each other on the same block. They usually walked to school together.

On the way to school one morning, Suzanne said, "Why don't you come to my house after school today? There's a neat program on TV, and we can work on the jigsaw puzzle I got for my birthday."

Barbara hadn't made any other plans, and besides, she liked Suzanne, so she agreed.

Barbara ate lunch with her friend Cindy that noon. As they were getting up to leave the lunchroom, Cindy asked, "Hey, why don't you come home with me after school? There's a new ice-cream parlor downtown, and my Mom promised she'd take me there. I had to bug her about it for days, and she finally said OK."

Ever since she'd first heard about the new ice-cream parlor, Barbara had wanted to go there. She loved ice cream, and so did Cindy. Barbara knew that Cindy's mom usually didn't take her on special trips after school.

# Barbara's Promise—Questions

1. What's Barbara's problem?
2. Should Barbara go home with Suzanne, or go with Cindy?
3. If Barbara agrees to go with Cindy, would she be breaking a promise she'd made to Suzanne?
4. If you were Suzanne, how would you feel if Barbara went with Cindy? Why?
5. Would it matter if Cindy was Barbara's best friend? Why or why not? What if Suzanne was someone Barbara really didn't like all that much?
6. Can you think of a situation in which it might be OK to break a promise?

# The Mouse Trap

Fred wondered what was going on around his friend Mark's locker. A bunch of kids were huddled in front of it, laughing and whispering. Fred looked more closely. Mark had hidden a mouse trap under a jacket in his locker. Whenever anyone passed by, he'd call out to them to come and look. Most of them just kept walking—Mark had a reputation for playing tricks.

"Come on, Tom!" Mark hollered out to one boy. "Take a look at what I've got. You'll like it, honest!"

Tom walked over. "Well, let's see, then!" he said.

"There's a full package of bubble gum under this jacket," Mark said, pointing to it. "Go ahead and take some."

Tom slid his hand under the jacket, and the trap just missed his fingers with a loud snap. He pulled his hand away quickly and yelled, "What is this, anyway?" Then he walked away down the hall in a hurry.

Mark and the others just laughed. Then Mark reset the trap and looked around for another victim.

Fred could see that someone could really get hurt by the trap. He also knew that the school rule against hurting others was strongly enforced. If a teacher found out what Mark was doing, Mark would probably be sent right home. That meant that his parents would be very angry. Fred knew that they'd punish him.

Fred didn't want anyone to get hurt, but he didn't want to tell on his friend and get him in trouble, either.

# The Mouse Trap—Questions

1. What should Fred do? Why?
2. What would be the best reason for Fred to tell on Mark?
3. How would Mark feel if Fred told on him?
4. Imagine that Fred had once done something wrong that Mark had known about, but Mark hadn't told on him. Would this make a difference to Fred?
5. What if Mark had told on Fred the time Fred had done something wrong? What then?
6. Can you think of a time when it might be better *not* to tell on someone?

# Getting Even

Brett was the kind of kid who held a grudge. Danny found that out one day when he accidentally got some paint on Brett's hand during art period. Brett wiped his brush on Danny's sleeve, called him a few names, and threatened to "get" him later.

By the time recess came around, Danny had almost forgotten the whole thing, but Brett hadn't. He had only started to get even with Danny. Brett spotted Danny on the playground and started chasing him. Danny saw him coming and tried to explain. "It was only an accident! I didn't mean to get paint on you!"

"You liar!" yelled Brett. "You did it on purpose, and I'm going to get you good! Just wait!"

He caught up with Danny and shoved him. Then he took the pencil sticking out of Danny's pocket and threw it over the fence.

"I'm not through with you yet!" Brett said, walking away. "Wait 'til after school!"

By now, Danny was convinced that Brett meant business. He was smaller than Brett and didn't want to get into a fight, so he decided to hurry home after school. But Brett was ready and waiting when Danny took his usual shortcut down an alley behind a grocery store. Suddenly, Brett jumped out from behind a wall, grabbed Danny's shirt, tearing it, and pushed Danny up against a door.

"Cut it out!" Danny hollered.

"What's the matter? You scared? Scared to fight?" Brett taunted. "Watch this!"

He took Danny's lunchbox and threw it on the ground. Then he jumped on it and laughed at the sound it made as he crushed it almost flat. Then Brett punched Danny in the stomach. He was aiming another punch at his face when Danny stepped to the side. Brett's empty swing threw him off balance, and he fell against a tall stack of wooden crates filled with apples. The crates crashed down on him and knocked over another stack which also came down, pinning Brett under a heavy pile.

"Owww, my arm! I think it's broken! Danny, help me! Get some help! Please!"

Danny wasn't sure whether or not he should help Brett.

## Getting Even—Questions

1. What's Danny's problem?
2. Should Danny help Brett? Why or why not? What is the right thing for him to do?
3. What's the best reason you can think of for Danny's helping Brett?
4. Would it make a difference if Danny had pushed Brett into the stack of crates? Why or why not?
5. Can you think of a situation in which it would be okay to get even with someone?
6. Do you always have to help people who need help? Why or why not?

# The Final Rehearsal

A group of kids decided to get together and put on a play. While they were choosing parts, Jay insisted that he wanted the lead and that if he couldn't have it he wouldn't be in the play at all. Jay was a pretty good actor, so the other kids let him have his way.

Their teacher found out about the play and asked the group if they'd like to perform for the monthly PTA meeting. They agreed and practiced even harder. Everything went smoothly—until the day of the final rehearsal.

On the day of the PTA meeting, everyone agreed to give up the half-hour lunch recess to practice. Everyone showed up but Jay. The others looked all over, but no one could find him. He had such an important part that the rehearsal was really a waste without him.

When Jay finally appeared in class after recess, the students in the play demanded to know where he'd been.

"Well, I wanted to play basketball in the lunchtime league. This was the day they chose teams," he shrugged.

Everyone agreed that Jay shouldn't have missed the rehearsal, but as they talked about it they all had different reasons why they thought Jay had been wrong. One person said that Jay had broken a promise. Someone else said that Jay had let them down—after all, they did give him the lead. Another person complained that the rehearsal time had been wasted.

# The Final Rehearsal—Questions

1. What's the problem here?
2. What's the best reason for saying that Jay was wrong for not showing up at the rehearsal?
3. How would Jay feel if the play was a flop and all the people in the audience laughed at them?
4. Jay decided that he could do whatever he wanted during recess. After all, that's what recess is for. Was he right?
5. Would it matter if Jay had had to choose between studying for a math test and going to rehearsal (instead of playing basketball)?

# Eddie and the Lunch Line

Eddie felt lucky. He had P.E. just before noon, and the gym was right next to the cafeteria, so if he hurried he could be among the first kids in line at the cafeteria door. It was the last day before summer vacation, and the school always served a special lunch on that day—hamburgers and ice-cream bars. Ice-cream bars were Eddie's favorite food. On days like this, the line got long fast.

Eddie managed to get near the head of the line. Eddie's friend Tom had to come all the way from a class at the other end of the building. There were over sixty kids waiting by the time Tom arrived.

Tom walked up to Eddie and said, "Let me in front of you, man. I'll give you my ice cream."

# Eddie and the Lunch Line—Questions

1. Should Eddie let Tom in line? Why or why not? What would be right?
2. What's the best reason why Eddie should let Tom in line?
3. What's the best reason why Eddie shouldn't let him in? Does it make a difference how many kids are in the line? Why or why not?
4. What will the kids in line behind Eddie think if he lets Tom in? Should this make a difference to Eddie?
5. Is "cutting in line" wrong? If so, what makes it wrong?
6. Can you think of a situation in which it might be okay to let someone cut in line in front of you?

# A Fight in the Park

Chad and two of his friends, Mary and Phil, were spending Saturday afternoon playing Frisbee in the park when they noticed two younger boys fighting. They looked like they were really going at it, too, and were making a lot of noise.

"Let's break up that fight," Phil suggested. "There must be a better way for them to settle their problems."

"No, wait," Chad said. "I think we should stay out of it. It's none of our business."

One of the younger boys finally got the better of the other and started kicking him. Mary sided with Phil. "Come on, let's break it up," she said. "Someone might get hurt if we don't."

"I still think we ought to mind our own business," Chad answered. "Nobody's going to get hurt. They're both too little to hurt each other. Let's go somewhere else and play."

He managed to convince Phil and Mary, and the three of them walked off to another part of the park.

# A Fight in the Park—Questions

1. Did Chad and his two friends do the right thing by not getting involved in the fight? Why or why not?
2. Was Chad's argument that they should "mind their own business" a good rule to follow? Why or why not?
3. Phil felt they should stop the fight because there are better ways to settle problems. Mary felt they should stop the fight because someone could get hurt. Which is the better reason? Why?
4. Would it make a difference if someone was already hurt in the fight? Why or why not?
5. Is there ever a time when it's best to "mind your own business"?

# No Girls Allowed?

The sixth-grade basketball club had a problem. Should they let Shelley, a girl, join their club?

The club had never let girls in before. They had played basketball together for a long time and were a good team. They got to use the school gym every Tuesday afternoon and sometimes even played sixth graders from other schools.

Club rules called for the boys to vote on new members. Everyone in the club could tell that Shelley knew a lot about basketball and played as well as they did. They'd often watched her playing with her older brother in the park. But she'd be the first girl in the club—and if she joined, then some of her friends might want to join, too. The boys really didn't want a lot of girls in their club. When it came time to vote, the boys in the basketball club didn't know what to do.

# No Girls Allowed?—Questions

1. What's the problem here?
2. How do you think the boys in the club should vote? What would be right? Why?
3. Is there anything wrong with a club that doesn't allow girls? What? Why?
4. Is there anything wrong with a club that doesn't allow boys? What? Why?
5. Suppose that the boys decide not to let Shelley join their club just because she's a girl, and Shelley complains to the principal. What would be the right thing for the principal to do?
6. Sometimes, people make rules that keep persons of different races or religious beliefs from joining certain clubs or groups. Are these kinds of rules any different from the one the boys' basketball club had?

# The Spelling Test

Every Wednesday morning, the teacher gave the sixth-grade class a spelling test—twenty-five words from their weekly lessons, and five hard bonus words. The highest scorer in the class was rewarded with an extra free period during the afternoon. Whenever April won the free period, she spent time in the art room. She was working on a special gift for her mother's birthday.

April and two of her friends, Mary and Lisa, sat close together in class. During this Wednesday's spelling test, April saw Mary slip a small piece of paper to Lisa. The paper had the five bonus words written on it. Mary had prepared it before the test.

When the scores were added up, April realized what her friends' cheating would mean. Lisa was the only person in the class to get all thirty words right. April had missed only one, a bonus word, and had the next best score. Mary had missed three of the regular words.

April had a decision to make. She felt that cheating was wrong—and besides, if she told on Mary and Lisa, she'd get the free period. At the same time, she didn't *want* to get her friends in trouble.

# The Spelling Test—Questions

1. Should April tell on Mary and Lisa? Why or why not? What is the right thing for April to do?
2. How would Lisa feel if April told on her? How would Mary feel? Should April think about how the other girls would feel when she is deciding the right thing to do?
3. Suppose there was no reward for spelling the most words right. Would this make a difference to April? Why or why not?
4. Suppose that Lisa wasn't April's friend. Would this make a difference? Why or why not?
5. Can you think of a situation in which it would be okay to cheat?
6. In general, do you think cheating is wrong? If yes, what is it that makes it wrong?

# What's a Friend?

Carrie's new friendship with Julie Maxy was becoming a problem for her. The Maxy family was the most disliked—in fact, the most hated—family in town. True, the Maxy house wasn't as nice and neat as others. (Cardboard covered a broken window, and an old dishwasher rusted in the front yard.) And it seemed like the five Maxy kids wore the same clothes to school almost every day. And they *did* act a little strange. But still, Carrie didn't think that they really deserved such a bad reputation. Other kids refused to talk to the Maxy kids in school, and they wouldn't even sit next to them or touch something one of them had touched.

Carrie thought that Julie Maxy was really a very nice person. Julie said strange things sometimes, but she was smart and funny and interesting to talk to. She read a lot and knew about many different things. Carrie was amazed that Julie never seemed to get angry at the other kids for treating her so badly.

Carrie's friends Jodi, Anne, and Heather were upset with her for being friendly to Julie. Anne was one of the most popular girls in school, and she thought it was stupid that Carrie had anything to do with Julie. At first she just teased Carrie, but finally Anne told Carrie that if she didn't stop talking to Julie she and the other girls wouldn't go around with Carrie anymore.

Carrie had to choose between Julie and her other friends. She didn't like to drop Julie, but in the end she did, because she chose to stay with Anne and her other friends. Carrie decided that Anne was right: Julie was a little bit weird. If all the other kids didn't like Julie, there must be some good reason.

# What's a Friend?—Questions

1. Should Carrie have stopped being friends with Julie? Why or why not? Did she do the right thing?
2. How do you think Carrie explained to Julie that she couldn't be her friend anymore?
3. Was Anne being a good friend by telling Carrie to drop Julie? Why or why not?
4. Do clothes or houses or the way someone looks have anything to do with friendship? Explain.
5. What makes a person a real friend?

# Eric's Secret

Eric was really worried. He'd seen Jesse take a library book from Carol's desk. Carol was looking for it frantically. Today was the last day to turn it in, and Jesse was absent. If Carol didn't turn her book in on time, she'd lose her library privileges.

Eric knew that Jesse had spent the night at his older sister's place, but Eric didn't know where Jesse's older sister lived. The only way Eric could think of to reach him was to call Jesse's parents. But Eric knew that Jesse's father often got mad at Jesse, even over little things. Sometimes he whipped Jesse with a belt. That's why Jesse often went to his sister's. Eric was sure that Jesse would really get it if his parents found out about the book.

# Eric's Secret—Questions

1. What is Eric's problem? What's the right thing for Eric to do?
2. How might Carol feel if she found out that Eric had known about the theft all along and hadn't told? What if she'd lost her library privileges?
3. Would it make any difference to Eric if Jesse was his best friend? If Carol was his best friend?
4. If Eric had told their teacher about Jesse, what should the teacher do?

# Cathy Is a Liar

Megan and her friends were getting very tired of having to put up with Cathy. Cathy liked to exaggerate, especially when she was talking about herself and how many boys liked her and what the teacher had written on her report card. But most of the other kids didn't call this exaggerating. They called it lying, and it made them mad.

One day, when Cathy told a really big whopper, some of the girls decided to teach her a lesson. They agreed to paint "CATHY IS A LIAR" inside of her locker where everyone would be sure to see. The next morning one of the girls brought a can of spray paint to school. The girls decided to paint Cathy's locker while everybody else was outside for recess. That way they wouldn't get caught.

Megan wasn't sure what to do. She didn't know if it would be right to paint Cathy's locker—even if Cathy *was* a liar—but her friends insisted. Megan knew that her friends would be mad at her if she didn't go along with them. Finally, she agreed to help paint the inside of Cathy's locker.

## Cathy Is a Liar—Questions

1. Was it right or wrong for Megan and her friends to paint the message in Cathy's locker? Why?
2. Did Cathy deserve what she got?
3. Should Megan tell Cathy about the message inside her locker before Cathy has a chance to open it?
4. Megan had at least three reasons for helping to paint the inside of Cathy's locker:
   - Cathy was telling stories that weren't true and deserved a lesson.
   - Megan's friends wanted Megan to go along with them.
   - Megan's friends would be mad at her if she didn't go along with them.

   Which of these reasons is the best one for painting the inside of Cathy's locker? Why?
5. When Cathy saw the message, her feelings were hurt and she told the teacher. All the girls were discovered. Megan excused her action by saying, "It wasn't my idea. They told me to help." Is this a good argument? Is it right or wrong? Why? Should Megan be punished as much as her friends?
6. What would be the best way for the girls to handle Cathy's lying?
7. Is it ever right to "teach someone a lesson"?

# The Chattering Teeth

Bill and his father had moved to town only three days ago. Bill was lonely at first, but he soon made friends with Craig, who lived across the street. Today Bill and Craig were hanging around the magic shop, looking at things.

As they were getting ready to leave, Craig said, "Go on outside and wait. I'll be out in a second."

While Craig and Bill were walking home, Craig pulled something out of his pocket.

"Look what I got," Craig said. It was a set of chattering teeth, still wrapped in shiny plastic.

"I didn't know you had any money with you," said Bill.

"I don't," replied Craig. "I swiped them." Then he added, "They don't cost much. Anyway, nobody'll notice that they're gone." He put the teeth in his mouth and clacked them at Bill.

Bill thought he should go back and tell the owner of the magic shop, but he didn't want to get his new friend in trouble.

# The Chattering Teeth—Questions

1. What's the right way to handle this problem?
2. Would it be right or wrong for Bill to tell on Craig?
3. What would Craig think of Bill if Bill told on him? Should this make a difference to Bill when he decides whether or not to tell?
4. Suppose that there'd been a sign inside the store which said, "SHOPLIFTERS WILL BE PROSECUTED. NO EXCEPTIONS." Would that make a difference to Bill?
5. Does it matter that the teeth were not expensive?
6. Most people feel that stealing is wrong. What exactly makes it wrong?
7. Can you think of a situation in which it would be all right to steal?

# Mailbox

Tammy and her friends always walked home from school together, and sometimes they did things that Tammy didn't think were quite right. She usually went along with her friends, though, because she didn't want them to think she was a spoilsport.

One day, Liz opened a mailbox along the street and started fooling around with the letters and junk mail inside. Tammy and the other girls thought it was funny, and soon they were all drawing mustaches on the people in the ads. They also changed some of the writing to make funny words and names out of the addresses.

Liz thought that all of this was just great and wanted to do it again the next day. She opened Mrs. McCracken's mailbox. Mrs. McCracken was a mean old lady who yelled at them whenever they walked too close to her plants. All the girls hated her, but Tammy thought that Liz was going a little too far when she opened a letter and started writing on the paper inside.

"Maybe you shouldn't do that, Liz," Tammy said. "That letter is personal."

"Come on, it's just Mrs. McCracken's. She's an old sourpuss. Remember the last time she hollered at us? She deserves it! You take a letter, too."

# Mailbox—Questions

1. What should Tammy do? Why?
2. Is Liz's argument that "Mrs. McCracken deserves it" a good one? Why or why not?
3. Suppose that Liz says, "I'll blame the whole thing on you, Tammy, if you back out now and we ever get caught." What should Tammy do in this case?
4. What if there was almost no chance that the girls would ever get caught? Should this make a difference to Tammy?
5. Should it make a difference if the girls only played around with the junk mail and didn't open any personal letters?

# The Reward

"Hey, look!" Laura pointed out to the other girls. "There's Mrs. Green trying to get all her groceries up the steps! Let's go help her." Heather, Ruth, and Laura all hurried over to carry Mrs. Green's bags for her.

"Here, we'll help you," Laura said, taking the heavy grocery bag out of Mrs. Green's hands. Each girl carried two bags up the long flight of stairs to the Greens' apartment. Mrs. Green was so grateful that she reached into one bag and pulled out a package of candy bars.

"You girls deserve a reward," she said, smiling.

The girls thanked her and went back across the street to divide up the candy.

Laura opened the package and said, "Well, there are four bars in here. I get to keep the extra one since it was my idea to help Mrs. Green."

"Wait a minute!" said Ruth. "We all carried two bags up the steps. We should share the fourth candy bar." Heather agreed with Ruth, but Laura wouldn't budge.

# The Reward—Questions

1. Is it right for Laura to keep the extra bar, or should the girls share it? Why?
2. Would it make a difference if Laura had carried two bags and the other girls had each carried only one? What if Laura had carried only one bag?
3. If Laura and her friends help Mrs. Green carry her groceries another time, should they expect to be rewarded?
4. In our society, should people who work the hardest make the most money?
5. Imagine a society in which everyone makes the same amount of money regardless of their jobs. Do you think that a society like this could work? Explain.

# Choosing Teams

It was Adam's turn to be a kickball-team captain. That meant that he and the captain of the other team would be picking their players. A coin was tossed, and Adam got first pick. He was glad about that until he looked at the line of players and realized that he had a problem. He wanted to pick his best friend, Kent, but Bob was a better player. Adam thought about it for a minute. Finally, he decided to pick Kent—even though he knew that Bob would have been better for the team.

## Choosing Teams—Questions

1. Was it right or wrong for Adam to pick Kent? Why?
2. Can Adam pick whomever he wants to play on his team—or does he owe it to the other players on his team to pick the best team he can?
3. What would happen if one team captain picked only his or her friends and the other team captain picked only the best players?
4. What are the fairest ways to pick teams? Explain.
5. Should even very poor players be allowed to play on teams?
6. What is the main purpose of a sport—to win or to have fun?

# Stick to Your Own Kind

One day after school, Michelle invited her friend Peggy to spend the next Friday night at her house. "I'll have to ask my parents first," Michelle said, "but I'm sure they'll say it's okay."

They didn't, though. "We don't like that you play with Peggy, and we don't think it's a good idea to have her stay over night here," her mother said. "Peggy belongs to a different race than we do. It's better to stick to your own kind."

Michelle didn't know what to do. She would have to tell Peggy something, but she didn't know what to say. She didn't want to hurt Peggy's feelings, so when she saw her in school the next day she said, "Peggy, about spending the night at my house . . . well, I got in trouble at home, and my parents won't let me have anyone over night for a long time." Peggy gave Michelle a funny look and just walked away.

## Stick to Your Own Kind—Questions

1. What was Michelle's problem?
2. Michelle didn't want to hurt Peggy's feelings, so she lied to her. Was this the right or the wrong thing to do? Why?
3. Suppose that Michelle decides to tell Peggy the truth. What would be the best way to explain the situation to her?
4. Maybe Peggy's "funny look" means that she knows why Michelle can't have her over to spend the night. Would it make a difference if Michelle were extra nice to her for the rest of the day?
5. Is there anything that Michelle can say to her parents to help them change their minds? What?

# Dilemmas with Parents

Problems children face in dealing with their parents' rules and opinions.

# Pam's Bike

Pam's family didn't have a lot of money. Her father had left three years ago, and he wasn't sending them anything to help out. Her mother worked, but she barely made enough money to support herself and her three children.

Pam had been working a paper route for a long time. She was saving her money for a new ten-speed bike. One day, Pam told her mother that she'd saved nearly $50. Her mother looked sad for a minute, and then she said, "Pam, I know you've wanted a bike for quite a while, and I know you've been working hard for it. But your little brothers need clothes. Jason's about worn his shoes out, and Ted's growing so fast that none of his clothes fit him anymore. The money I made this month has to go for rent and doctor bills."

# Pam's Bike—Questions

1. What's Pam's problem?
2. What should she do with her money?
3. Does Pam's mother have a right to ask her for the money Pam earned by herself?
4. What if Pam's mother wanted to use the money for something unnecessary? Should Pam have a say about what her money will be used for?
5. Do parents have the right to control their children's property? Why or why not?
6. Should children always do what their parents ask them to do? Why or why not?

# Steve's Leaving Home

Steve's parents both drank too much, and it was hard on him. He was always glad when he could get out of the house. He even liked going to school, and he spent as much time as he could at his friends' houses.

Whenever she was drunk, Steve's mother would lose her temper and scream at him. She said ugly things about him, about his clothes, his hair, and anything else she could think of. Steve's father did the same thing. When he wasn't arguing with Steve's mother, he was giving Steve a bad time. Sometimes he would even hit Steve, and when this happened Steve just left the house for a while until things cooled off.

Steve's parents' drinking seemed to get worse, and Steve thought more and more about leaving the house for good—running away. He figured that it wouldn't matter to his parents. They probably didn't want him around anyway.

One night, both his mother and father got drunk. They started fighting with each other and yelling at him. Steve tried to get them to stop, but this only made his father angrier. Finally, he slapped Steve in the face, knocking him down.

Steve decided that was the last time he would let it happen. He would run away the next day.

# Steve's Leaving Home—Questions

1. Did Steve make the right decision? Why or why not?
2. Do Steve's parents have a right to treat him the way they do? Why or why not?
3. Suppose a neighbor knew what was going on. Should he or she report Steve's parents to the police or other authorities? Why or why not?
4. Would Steve be treating his parents fairly if he ran away? Why or why not?
5. If Steve knew that alcoholism is a disease, should that make any difference to him? What could he decide to do in that case?
6. Do children ever have the right to tell their parents what to do? Do children have a right to leave home?

# A Deal's a Deal

"Please, Tim, don't tell 'em! Please!"

"They'll find out anyway."

"Not if you don't tell 'em! And even if they do find out, they don't have to know I did it. It wasn't my fault. It was just an accident!"

Tim's little brother, Scotty, was pleading with him not to tell their parents about the scratch his bike had made on the side of their car. The bike had fallen against the car because Scotty hadn't set the kickstand properly.

Tim ran his fingers over the scratch. It had taken the paint right off for about three inches.

"It is too your fault," Tim said. "Dad told you to park your bike away from the car. He was mad when it fell on the lawn chair last summer and dented it. You'll really get it for this."

"Look," Scotty answered. "I'll make you a deal. You don't tell 'em about the scratch, and I won't tell 'em that you lost your new jacket."

Tim had carelessly left his new jacket at the movie theater on Saturday afternoon. He hadn't known how to tell his parents about it.

"Okay," answered Tim. "It's a deal. I won't tell, but you'd better not tell on me, either."

Later that evening their father asked Tim about the scratch on the car. At first, Tim didn't answer. Finally, he couldn't avoid the question any longer.

"Tim, I want you to tell me if you know anything about how the car got scratched," his father said sternly.

Tim thought to himself, "A deal's a deal." Then he said out loud to his father, "Honest, Dad, I don't know."

# A Deal's a Deal—Questions

1. What's Tim's problem?
2. Did Tim do the right thing by keeping the deal he made with his brother? Why or why not? Did he do the right thing by making the deal in the first place?
3. What if Tim's father blamed him for the scratch on the car? Should that make a difference to Tim?
4. What if Scotty got in trouble for something else that same evening and told his parents that Tim had lost his jacket?
5. Can you think of a time when it might be wrong to tell your parents the truth?

## Stacey Goes to the Movies

Stacey wanted to go to a movie that her parents didn't want her to see. Her friend Jenny wanted to see it, too, and Jenny's parents didn't like the idea either. So Stacey told her parents that she was going over to Jenny's house, and Jenny told her parents that she was going over to Stacey's house. Then the two girls went to the movie.

When Stacey's parents found out, Stacey admitted that she had been wrong to lie. But she didn't think that the punishment her parents gave her was fair—no movies at all for three months.

# Stacey Goes to the Movies—Questions

1. Stacey thought that she'd been wrong to lie to her parents. Do you agree with her? Why or why not? Was she also wrong to go to the movie against their wishes even if she had not lied?
2. Is it right for parents to choose the movies their children should see? At what age do you think children should be able to make their own choices?·
3. Is it right for Stacey's parents to punish her for what she did? Why or why not?
4. Do you agree with Stacey that the punishment isn't fair? Why or why not?
5. Do you think that punishments do any good? How much good do they do?
6. How can you decide whether a punishment is fair or not?
7. Do you think that children have the right to decide how they should be punished if they do something wrong?
8. Should parents be allowed to spank, paddle, or in any other way hurt their children as punishment?

# Amy

Judge Bennett didn't like deciding on divorce cases. He found it hard to deal with the problems of families who were breaking up. It was especially hard when children were involved.

The judge wasn't looking forward to the hearing involving nine-year-old Amy and her family. Amy's mother and father were divorcing, and they were fighting over who should get to keep Amy. Judge Bennett tried to consider the whole situation fairly. Amy had been living with her mother during her parents' separation, and the judge knew that Amy wanted to go on living with her mother. But he also knew that Amy's mother often neglected her. Amy made most of her own meals, was home alone much of the time, and seldom had clean clothes to wear. Amy insisted that she would be unhappy if she had to live with her father. She wanted to live with her mother in spite of the way her mother neglected her.

During the hearing, Judge Bennett decided that Amy's mother was not able to care for Amy properly and that she would be better off with her father.

# Amy—Questions

1. What was Judge Bennett's problem?
2. Do you think that his decision was right or wrong? Why?
3. Do you think that judges should listen to kids when deciding on cases like this one? Why or why not?
4. Should kids ever be allowed to make decisions like this for themselves? Why or why not?

# Holly's Choice

Holly and her older brother Jeff were best friends besides being brother and sister. They talked about almost everything, including boyfriends and girlfriends.

When school started in September, Jeff started hanging around with some new kids. Not long after, he began to lose weight, and his personality started changing. He had always been a happy-go-lucky person who liked sports and had a lot of friends. Now he was always nervous and upset, and he spent a lot of time alone in his room. His parents were very worried about him. At dinner, they'd often ask him what was wrong, but he'd tell them that they were just being "pushy" and "nosy" and that there was nothing wrong with him at all.

Late one night, Holly went into Jeff's room to talk. She asked him why he seemed so different. Jeff started crying and said that he was taking drugs. The other kids he hung around with were doing it, and he'd gotten involved, too. He said that the drugs made him feel good and kept him from thinking about his problems but that he felt sick when he couldn't get any. He made Holly promise not to tell anyone what he'd said—especially their parents. He promised to stop taking the drugs as soon as he was able to.

The next day, Holly's mother came to her and said, "Dad and I are very worried about Jeff. He's changed a lot during these past few weeks, and we don't know why. You and Jeff have always talked about everything. What's the matter with him lately? It's important that you tell me the truth."

# Holly's Choice—Questions

1. What's Holly's problem?
2. What is the right thing for Holly to do? Why?
3. How would Jeff feel if Holly told their parents what she knew?
4. What if drug users in Holly's state had to go to jail? Should that make a difference to Holly?
5. Holly had once read a newspaper story about a boy Jeff's age who'd died from drug abuse. What if Holly believed that Jeff might die, too?
6. Can you think of a time when it might be okay to keep a promise like Holly made to her brother?

# The Broken Promise

Dana's mother had promised her that if she got all of the problems on her math test right for three weeks in a row, she could have a slumber party for her birthday. Dana studied hard and finally brought her third perfect test home to show her mother.

"I did it!" she said proudly. "Now can I have my slumber party?"

"I'm glad you did so well in math," her mother answered, "but I'm afraid I've changed my mind. I don't think it's a good idea to have any parties right away. The new carpeting in the living room might get damaged. I'm sorry—but I never should have promised you a slumber party in the first place."

Dana was very angry about this. After all, she'd kept her part of the bargain, and now her mother was backing down. Dana decided to get even with her mother by not doing the jobs she usually did around the house. When it was time to clear the dishes off the dinner table, Dana made excuses and went to her room. Then she "forgot" to make her bed the next morning. And when Dana's mother asked her to take out the garbage, Dana ignored her.

# The Broken Promise—Questions

1. Was it right for Dana to "get even" with her mother? Why or why not?
2. Was Dana's mother right or wrong when she changed her mind about the slumber party? Why?
3. How could Dana's mother have explained the situation to help Dana understand her decision?
4. What if Dana's mother had come up with another idea for a birthday party? Would that have made a difference to Dana?
5. Dana's mother broke a promise she'd made to Dana. Was this right or wrong?
6. Is it ever right to break a promise? When? Why?
7. Is it worse for a parent to break a promise made to a child than it is for a child to break a promise made to a parent? Why or why not?

# John's Father

John's father didn't like Mexican-American people. Whenever he talked about them, he called them insulting names. He told John that if he ever caught him playing with Mexican-American kids, John would be in big trouble.

No one at John's school seemed to pay much attention to race or nationality. Most kids had friends with different backgrounds. When John was younger, he hadn't had any Mexican-American friends, so his father's attitude hadn't been a problem for him. As he got older, though, he began to realize that his father's rule might mean that he wouldn't have any friends at all.

John had been friends with Dave and Ben for as long as he could remember. One day, they asked him to be on the basketball team they were organizing for the school league. Dave had already asked Antonio and Miguel to join the team, and they had agreed to. John thought about his father's rule, and then he thought about how much he wanted to play ball with his friends.

## John's Father—Questions

1. What's John's problem?
2. Should John join the team anyway? Why or why not?
3. If it weren't for his father's rule, John wouldn't care what race or nationality his friends belonged to. What's the best argument John could use to say that he should be allowed to play on the team?
4. Should John join the team without telling his father? Why or why not?
5. Can you think of a time when it might be okay to break a rule your parents made?

# Pete's Bedtime

Pete and his family had recently moved to the city from a small farming community. While they were living on the farm, Pete's father made all the kids go to bed at seven o'clock every evening. They all had to get up early to help out on the farm, so none of the kids really minded much. In the city, it was different. Pete's father was working in a factory, so there weren't any farm chores to do in the mornings. Pete knew that most of his new school friends got to go to bed anywhere between eight and ten—and some even stayed up later. Pete thought that it was unfair for his father to still insist on his going to bed at seven.

On Friday, Pete's new friend Shawn invited him to spend the night at his house. Pete asked his father if it was okay, and his father said that he could go only if he promised to go to bed at seven. Pete agreed. When he arrived at Shawn's house, Shawn said, "There's a great show on TV tonight. It starts at eight. My mom promised to make popcorn for us while we watch it."

"I don't think I should stay up that late," Pete answered. "When I'm at home, I have to go to bed at seven. My Dad said that I could spend the night here only if I promised to go to bed at my regular time."

"That's silly," Shawn's mother called out from the kitchen. "You're old enough to stay up later than seven. You boys enjoy the show, and, Pete, I won't say a word to your father."

# Pete's Bedtime—Questions

1. What's Pete's problem?
2. Should he go to bed at seven anyway? Why or why not?
3. What's a proper bedtime for a nine or ten year old? How about an eleven or twelve year old? Who should decide?
4. Is Pete's father right in making him go to bed at seven every night? What argument could Pete use to get his father to change his mind?
5. Is Shawn's mother right in encouraging Pete to stay up past his bedtime? Why or why not?
6. If parents and children disagree about something, what's a good way to solve the problem?

# A Letter from School

Erin had been brought up to respect other people's property. She knew that it was wrong to take things that didn't belong to her, and once when she'd borrowed a record from her friend Melissa and scratched it, she'd paid for it out of her own money.

She also knew that it was wrong to open someone else's mail. "Mail is private," her mother had said. "We won't open yours, and we don't want you to open ours, either." Now Erin was feeling as if she'd have to break that rule.

Someone had been writing on the walls at school, and Erin had been accused of doing it. She'd just been looking at the writing and had happened to have a pen in her hand when the principal had walked by and seen her. Erin tried to explain, but the principal's mind was made up. He'd told her that he was going to write a letter to Erin's parents about it. The letter would say that Erin would be suspended if it ever happened again.

Erin knew that even though her parents usually believed her, a letter from school would be hard to explain. She might not be able to convince them that she was telling the truth in time to go to her friend Marly's party that weekend. She didn't want to miss the party—and she didn't want her parents to think even for a minute that she was lying to them.

Erin checked the mail every day before her parents came home from work. On Friday afternoon, the letter arrived from school. Erin felt guilty about it, but she opened the letter anyway. It said what the principal had told her it would say—that Erin had been writing on the walls and that she'd be suspended if it ever happened again. It didn't say anything about Erin's parents having to answer the letter or call the principal about it.

So Erin tore the letter up into small pieces and buried the pieces in the trash can.

## A Letter from School—Questions

1. What was Erin's problem?
2. Do you think that what Erin did was right or wrong? Why?
3. What if the letter had said that Erin's parents should schedule a conference with the principal? Would that have made a difference to Erin?
4. What if Erin's parents sometimes opened Erin's mail? Should that have made a difference to Erin?
5. What if Erin really had written on the walls at school? Would that have made the fact that she opened the letter more right or more wrong? Why?
6. If Erin had just thrown the letter away without opening it first, would that have made a difference? Why or why not?
7. Remember that opening someone else's mail is against the law. Should that have made a difference to Erin?
8. Can you think of a time when it might be okay to open someone else's mail?

# Crazy Ideas, Crazy Clothes

Larry likes rock music better than he likes almost anything else.

Larry's parents don't approve of his musical tastes. They think that rock music is bad for Larry and other kids who listen to it. Larry's tried to explain why he likes the music, but his parents don't understand.

"Rock music gives kids crazy ideas," his father likes to say. "It makes them wear crazy clothes and do crazy things. Look at the rock musicians! Look at the way they dress. Look at their hair!"

"I certainly don't want any son of mine taking drugs or running around with hippies," Larry's mother agrees. "Rock music causes a lot of the problems in the world today."

Larry has a record player, and he wants to buy some rock records, but his parents won't let him. Larry makes his own money mowing lawns, and he feels that he should be allowed to buy records if he wants to. He thinks that his parents' ban on rock music is unfair.

# Crazy Ideas, Crazy Clothes—Questions

1. Is it right or wrong for Larry's parents to forbid him to buy rock records? Why?
2. Larry earns his own spending money. Should he be able to do what he wants with it?
3. What if Larry's parents were giving him an allowance, and Larry didn't earn his own money? Would that make a difference?
4. Should Larry buy the records anyway and not tell his parents? Why or why not?
5. Do parents have the right to control the things their children can and can't buy? What about books? Magazines? Clothes? Guns? Cigarettes? Drugs? Liquor?
6. Can you think of a time when it might be okay for a child to go against his or her parents' wishes?
7. Try to think of a method that Larry and his parents could use to agree on what is good or bad for him to buy.

# Dilemmas in History

Problems faced by people in the past.

# Nathan Hale

Nathan Hale was born in 1755. He was only twenty-one years old when he was hung by the British during the American Revolution.

Nathan Hale was a member of a small fighting group called the Rangers. When General George Washington wanted a volunteer to pass through the British lines to get information about the British army, he went to the Rangers. Hale volunteered. He disguised himself as a Dutch schoolmaster and succeeded in crossing the British lines where he gathered information. When he tried to return to the American lines, however, he was captured and hung the next day. Many people believe that Hale's own cousin, a Loyalist, betrayed him to the British. A Loyalist, or Tory, was someone who was in favor of the King of England and the British rule of the American Colonies.

According to tradition, Nathan Hale's last words before he was executed were, "I only regret that I have but one life to lose for my country." Hale is remembered as a hero because of his bravery and those famous words.

# Nathan Hale—Questions

1. Suppose that it was Nathan Hale's cousin who turned him in. Was that right or wrong? Why? Suppose that the person who turned him in was not related to Hale. Would that make a difference? Why?

2. What if Nathan Hale had been a Loyalist and his cousin had been an American soldier? Would we still consider Nathan Hale a hero?

3. If you were British, would you still think that Nathan Hale was a hero?

4. What if you found out that a member of your own family was a criminal? What if your own cousin, or brother, or sister had murdered someone, or was dealing in drugs, or was a spy for a foreign government? What would be the right thing for you to do?

5. Is it ever right to turn someone over to the authorities if there's a chance that the person will be executed?

# The Underground Railroad

Before the Civil War, it was against the law to help slaves escape. The law declared that anyone who aided fugitive (escaped) slaves would be punished. Some people didn't believe that black people should be slaves. These people set up a system called the Underground Railroad to help slaves from the Southern states reach safety in the Northern states and Canada. It wasn't really a railroad but got its name because railroad terms were used as code words. Escape routes between the South and the North were called "lines," stopping places (often people's homes) were called "stations," escaped slaves were called "packages" or "freight," and the people who led them along the "lines" were called "conductors." It was called "underground" because it was illegal and had to be kept secret.

Harriet Tubman was one famous "conductor." She had been a slave herself before she escaped. Tubman made nineteen successful trips into the South to help other slaves escape. Huge rewards were offered for her capture. The Quaker-church leader Thomas Garrett, another famous conductor, is said to have helped nearly three thousand slaves to reach freedom.

# The Underground Railroad—Questions

1. Remember that it was against the law to help slaves escape. Was it right or wrong for people like Harriet Tubman and Thomas Garrett to break the law by providing transportation and hiding places for escaped slaves?
2. If you'd been alive back then and had seen a slave, what do you think you would have done? Why? What would you have done if your parents owned slaves?
3. Harriet Tubman even managed to bring her own parents to freedom. If you'd been alive back then, would it have made a difference to you if a fugitive had been a relative or a close friend of yours?
4. People who were caught helping slaves had to pay heavy penalties. What if you'd known about a fugitive who needed help, and that person had been someone you didn't like?
5. Did the Southern slaveowner who owned Harriet Tubman have any right to get her back?
6. Should human beings ever own other human beings? Is slavery itself right or wrong? Why?

# The Depression

The Great Depression in the United States was a terrible time for many people, and 1932 was one of the worst years of the Depression. Some businesses were unable to keep going, so many people had no jobs and no money. Some people lost their homes. Parents worried that they wouldn't be able to feed their children. Cases were reported of people eating wild roots and weeds, of people taking scraps of food from garbage cans, of people living in railroad cars and under bridges. Some people decided that stealing was the only way to stay alive.

## The Depression—Questions

1. If something like the Depression happened again, and you found yourself without food or money, would you think that it was right or wrong to steal food for your family? Why?
2. What if you'd been a police officer during the Depression and had seen someone stealing food? Would you have arrested that person?
3. Imagine that you are living during the Depression. Your family is starving, and you can't get a job. You decide that you must steal some food. The store owner tries to stop you. Would it be right or wrong to hurt the store owner in order to get the food?

# Rosa Parks

On a December day in 1955, Rosa Parks, a black woman, was riding a bus in Montgomery, Alabama. When all the seats in the bus had been taken, and still more people were getting on, the driver told Rosa to stand up so that a white man could have her seat. This was a common practice in the South, and it was against the law to refuse to do what the bus driver said.

Rosa was tired and she did not want to give up her seat. So she refused to budge. She was arrested at the next stop, and this situation developed into the famous Montgomery bus boycott.

## Rosa Parks—Questions

1. Did Rosa do the right thing by refusing to give the white man her seat? Why or why not?
2. What if the driver had asked a black man to give up his seat to a white woman? Would that have made the situation any different?
3. During the bus boycott that followed Rosa Parks' arrest, many blacks refused to ride the city buses. They said that they wouldn't ride them until they were treated just as whites were and could sit wherever they pleased. The bus company lost a lot of business during the boycott and went into debt. Is it right or wrong to hurt a company or business in this way?
4. Some laws are discriminatory. That means that they treat some people differently than they treat others. Today, many women who have the same jobs as men aren't paid as much as the men are. Is this discriminatory? Write a law that would make any type of discrimination illegal.

# The Donner Party

During the 1800's, people from the eastern part of the United States began to move westward into California and Oregon. The Oregon Trail, the California Trail, and the Old Spanish Trail became established during the 1840's, and each year more groups set out to complete the long journey before the winter snows blocked the mountain passes.

One group, led by George Donner, left the California Trail for what they thought would be a shortcut. Nearly ninety people separated from a larger party at Fort Bridger in July, 1846, to try a more direct route south of the Great Salt Lake. They had many problems along the way, and it was late fall by the time they reached the Sierra Nevada mountains. By that time, heavy snows had fallen, and the people camped near what's now called Donner Lake.

On December 16, when the food supplies had nearly run out, ten men and five women set out on snowshoes to cross the mountains. They struggled through a month of cold, storms, and snow, with little food. Eight of the men died, and the survivors were so hungry that they ate the dead people. Two men and all of the women managed to get through to the Sacramento Valley.

Rescue parties set out to bring back the others who were camped by the lake, but those who were sick or injured had to be left behind. They ate dogs and cowhides and finally resorted to cannibalism, too. Only about half of the Donner Party lived to see California.

# The Donner Party—Questions

1. What were the problems that the Donner Party had?
2. Was it right or wrong for the survivors to eat the bodies of the people who died? Why?
3. Some people follow religions that say that bodies of dead people have to be properly buried. Should this make a difference to the survivors? Why or why not?
4. Would it ever be right to kill a person for food in order for a larger group to survive?
5. Imagine that a group of ten people has been shipwrecked. There's only enough food to keep five of them alive until a rescue ship comes. Should the food go to the five youngest people, or should it be divided equally? What if it was likely that everyone would die if the food were distributed equally?
6. Some people choose to become vegetarians. They don't eat meat because they feel that it's wrong to kill and eat animals. Do you agree or disagree? What's the difference between eating animal flesh and eating human flesh?

# Dilemmas in Society and the Law

Problems involving the law, other people, and other people's property.

# Doug and Matt

One day, Doug and Matt got into trouble at school. It all started when a boy named Eric called Doug names earlier in the day. Doug hated being called names, and at recess he decided to teach Eric a lesson. He caught Eric and knocked him down. Then he started beating him up. Matt, Doug's best friend, saw what was happening and decided to help Doug out, so he came over and started beating up on Eric, too.

The principal heard about it and called all three of the boys into her office. She decided that Doug and Matt would have to be punished, but not Eric.

"Doug, you have to stay after school today. Matt, you have to stay after school both today *and* tomorrow. What you did was even worse than what Doug did. Eric didn't call you names, so you didn't have any reason to hurt him. And Eric, I don't ever again want to hear that you called anyone names. If I do, then you'll have to stay after school, too."

# Doug and Matt—Questions

1. Was the principal's decision fair? Or should Doug and Matt get the same punishment? Why or why not?
2. Should Doug and Matt be punished at all for what they did? Why or why not?
3. Should Eric be punished, too? Why or why not?
4. Think of some names that people call each other. Why do you think people call each other names in the first place?
5. Is it right or wrong to call people names? Can you think of a situation in which it might be right?
6. Write a rule or set of rules for your school that would help to deal with situations like this one.

# The Boycott

Kevin's mother was involved in many political and social causes. She believed in helping people. Recently, she'd decided to boycott all products made by the Winter Foods Company. (When you *boycott* a product, you refuse to buy it.) She explained to Kevin that Winter Foods treated their workers very badly. The working conditions at the company were unsafe and unhealthy, and the workers got paid very little. The workers' union was asking people to boycott the company's products to force the company to make improvements.

"The brand of popcorn you like best is made by Winter Foods," Kevin's mother told him. "If you buy a different brand the next time you go to the store, that might help put pressure on the company." Kevin decided to switch to another brand.

Kevin spent weekends and Monday nights with his father, who was separated from his mother. One Monday night, Kevin invited several of his friends over to watch the football game on his father's new TV. About half an hour before Kevin's friends were due to arrive, Kevin's father discovered that they were out of popcorn and sent Kevin to the store to buy some.

When Kevin went to the store, he found that the only brand they had was Winter Foods. There was no time to go to another store, and besides, his father didn't agree with "all this boycott stuff." He would think that Kevin was silly if he came home without any popcorn just because of the boycott. So Kevin bought the popcorn and returned just before his friends arrived.

# The Boycott—Questions

1. What was Kevin's problem when he went into the grocery store?
2. Should he have bought the popcorn? Why or why not?
3. Kevin's father would probably say, "Your seventy-nine cents isn't going to make any difference to a big corporation." Do you agree or disagree?
4. If Kevin had been staying at his mother's house when he went to buy the popcorn, do you think he would have made the same decision? Why or why not?

# Teapot Lake

While vacationing at Teapot Lake, Erica, her brother Bill, and his friend John decided to spend a whole day exploring an island in the middle of the lake. Erica and Bill's father took them out in his boat in the morning and told them that he'd return for them before dinnertime.

Just before noon, Bill fell and cut his leg. It bled badly, and it was obvious to the children that they couldn't wait until their father returned to get help.

John spotted a boathouse down by the beach and ran to see if anyone was there. No one was. There was nothing inside the boathouse but a rowboat. When he came back and told Erica about what he'd found, Erica suggested that they take the boat and row Bill across the lake to their cottage. Then it would only take them about ten minutes to get help for Bill.

John said, "We can't do that. The boathouse is locked."

"We can break the window and open the door from the inside," Erica suggested.

"But that's against the law!" John exclaimed. "We could get into a lot of trouble if we did that!"

"There isn't time to argue," Erica said. Then she ran to the boathouse, broke the window, crawled inside, and opened the door. She pulled the rowboat down to the shore and waited for John to help Bill into it.

# Teapot Lake—Questions

1. What did Erica see the problem as being? How about John?
2. Was what Erica did right or wrong? Why?
3. Do Erica and John have a duty to help Bill? Why or why not?
4. What rights do the owners of the boathouse have in this situation? If the owners had been there, would they have had a duty to help the children? Why or why not?
5. Suppose John had convinced Erica not to break into the boathouse and Bill bled to death. Would John and Erica have been responsible for Bill's death?
6. Can you think of a time when helping someone out might be more important than obeying a rule or law?

# Loose Change

During intermission, Jody and Kim headed straight for the pop machine in the lobby of the movie theater.

"Hey, look at this!" Jody said excitedly, reaching into the coin return slot. "Somebody forgot their change! There's twenty-five cents here—enough for a candy bar!"

"Wait a minute," Kim said. "Maybe it belongs to that little boy over there. He was walking away from the pop machine just as we were coming out the door of the theater."

"Forget it! Finders keepers!" Jody said.

## Loose Change—Questions

1. Is it right or wrong for Jody to keep the money? Why?
2. What reasons can you think of that would make it okay for Jody to keep the money?
3. How many times have you heard someone say, "Finders keepers!"? Is that rule usually a good one? Why or why not?
4. If the little boy did leave the money in the machine, does he have a right to expect that someone will return it to him?
5. What if Kim had seen an adult walk away from the machine instead of the little boy? Would that make any difference?
6. What's the best reason you can think of for believing that Jody should return the money?
7. When is it okay to keep something you find?

# A Matter of Life or Death

Imagine for a minute that you and another person are being held captive by a madman. He has a gun. He looks at you and says, "I'm either going to kill you or the other person. You decide. The person who isn't shot gets to walk away free."

## A Matter of Life or Death—Questions

1. What kind of choice would you make in this situation?
2. What do you think is the right choice to make? Why? What makes it right?
3. What if the other person were your best friend, or your brother or sister, or your mother or father, or some other person close to you? Would this make a difference?
4. What if more than two people were being held captive, and the gunman promised to let three, four, or more of them go free if you chose to let him shoot you?

# Missy

Missy loved animals. Usually, this love brought her a great deal of satisfaction and enjoyment. She had a dog of her own, two cats, a turtle, and a mouse. She had a lot of fun with them, and she liked to take good care of them.

Once, though, Missy's love for animals caused a problem for her. An older man who lived next door to her had a dog. Missy knew that he treated the dog badly. He kept it tied up all the time, didn't feed it properly, and never kept it clean. He often beat the dog when he was angry—and Missy could hear the dog whining whenever the old man approached it.

Whenever she put her eye up close to the backyard fence, Missy could see the dog. Each time she peered through the fence, the dog looked more miserable. Missy worried about the dog. She was afraid that it might die.

Finally, Missy couldn't stand it any longer. She decided that she had to do something to help the dog. One evening, when she knew that her neighbor was gone, Missy went into his yard and untied the dog. She was glad to see it run off down the alley.

The dog never came back. For a long time afterward, the old man complained bitterly about the "dirty sneak" who stole his dog.

# Missy—Questions

1. What was Missy's problem? Was it really *her* problem? Why or why not?
2. Was what Missy did right or wrong? Why?
3. Would it have been better if Missy had reported the old man to the police or the ASPCA (American Society for the Prevention of Cruelty to Animals) instead of letting the dog go? Why or why not?
4. Can a person do anything he or she likes to a dog? What about a cat? A turtle? A fish? A snake? A snail? An ant? Is any one of these animals different from the others? Why or why not?
5. Many laboratories and corporations experiment on animals. They use mice, rabbits, dogs, cats, monkeys, and other animals to test the effects of diseases and new drugs. Sometimes they infect an animal with a disease and then wait to see what will happen to it. Other times they give chemicals to an animal and then watch its reactions. Researchers use what they learn from experimenting on animals when making decisions on what's good for human beings and what isn't. They believe that by experimenting on animals they can save human lives. Is this right or wrong? Why?
6. How are the rights of animals different from the rights of human beings?

# Robert Lyons

On a December evening in 1957, Robert Lyons and
two friends played cards at another friend's house in
Cleveland. After leaving the house, they decided that
they'd been cheated by their host and returned to get
their money back. They tied up the man and his wife
and stole money and several guns from them.

The man finally freed himself and called the
police. Later, when a police officer stopped the car the
three men were riding in, one of Lyons' friends jumped
from the car and ran. The other sat quietly, apparently
resigned to his arrest. But Robert Lyons drew a gun,
stepped out of the car, and shot the policeman in the
head, killing him.

Lyons was tried for first-degree murder, found
guilty, and condemned to the electric chair. He died
there in February, 1960.


## Robert Lyons—Questions

1. Was it right or wrong for the court to condemn Lyons to death
   because he'd killed the policeman? Why?
2. What if Lyons had killed someone other than a
   policeman—such as a person who was just walking along the
   street, or another criminal, or a child? Should that have made
   any difference?
3. What if Lyons had killed more than one person? Should that
   have made any difference?
4. What if the policeman had been your father? If you had been
   on the jury trying the case, would this have made a difference
   to you?
5. What if Robert Lyons had been your father? What then?
6. When someone receives the death penalty, this is called
   *capital punishment.* Do you think that capital punishment is
   right or wrong? Why?

# Sneakin' In

"Oh, no! I must have left it at home!"

Dave was really mad. After walking all day to the ball game with his friend Ted, he discovered that he'd forgotten to bring his money. Ted had just enough to pay for his own ticket.

"Let's sneak in," Ted suggested.

"I don't think we should," Dave answered.

"Look," Ted said, "it wouldn't be like you were taking someone else's seat or anything. There are always a lot of empty seats. We walked all the way here, and I want to see the game. But I don't want to watch it all by myself."

## Sneakin' In—Questions

1. What's David's problem?
2. What would be the right thing for David to do in this situation? Why?
3. Ted gave Dave three arguments for sneaking in. They were: A) They'd walked all the way there already. B) There are always empty seats. C) He didn't want to watch the game all by himself. Which is the best argument to justify sneaking in? Why? Can you think of any other arguments for sneaking in?
4. Think of some arguments Dave could use to persuade Ted that it would be wrong to sneak in. Which is the best argument? Why?
5. What if the boys had enough money to pay their way in but decided to sneak in anyway? Would this make any difference? Why or why not?
6. Can you think of a time when it might be okay to get into a game or some other event without paying?

# Vandalism

Vandalism is damaging or wrecking someone's property. A study of crime in Ohio during the 1960's and 1970's has shown that vandalism is the most common crime in that state. When six hundred tenth-grade students were asked questions about vandalism, 68 percent of the boys and 37 percent of the girls said that they had done acts of vandalism at one time or another.

It was found that most of the tenth-graders who'd done acts of vandalism thought of them as "games" instead of crimes. The vandalism they'd taken part in was generally something like painting on mailboxes or buildings. However, it also included breaking windows and damaging cars, shrubs, and other kinds of property.

Twelve percent of the students questioned said that they'd done what they'd done to "get even" with the owner of the property.

## Vandalism—Questions

1. What do you think of this study? Does it surprise you? Why or why not?
2. Do you think of vandalism as "just a game"? Explain.
3. Is vandalism always wrong? Is it ever right to damage someone else's property?
4. If you saw a good friend of yours damaging school property, would you report him or her? Why or why not?
5. Some people say that vandalism is wrong because it's against the law. Others say that it's wrong because it harms people or their property. Which is the best reason? Why?

# Alicia

Alicia didn't know what to do. Her little brother had been in an accident and needed an operation in order to walk again. The operation would cost two thousand dollars. Alicia's family didn't have two thousand dollars. They'd already tried borrowing the money, but they'd only been able to come up with half. The hospital wouldn't do the operation without getting the money first.

There seemed to be only one way out. On Wednesdays, Alicia did housecleaning for the Farrell family. They were well off and kept a lot of cash around the house. Alicia thought that the Farrells were mean. They had refused to loan her money when she'd told them about her brother and the operation. Alicia didn't want to steal from the Farrells. She'd never stolen anything in her life, and she was afraid that she'd lose her job and maybe even go to jail if she was caught. She didn't want to embarrass her family, either, but she couldn't stop thinking about her brother. That Wednesday, when she went to the Farrells', she waited until they'd left and then stole the money her family needed.

# Alicia—Questions

1. What was Alicia's problem?
2. Was what she did right or wrong? Why?
3. What if Alicia didn't like her brother? Should that make a difference? What if the money was needed for someone she didn't even know?
4. Were the Farrells right or wrong to refuse to lend her the money? Was the hospital right or wrong to refuse to do the operation until Alicia's family had the money?
5. Can you think of a time when it might be right to steal?
6. What if Alicia's brother had been so sick that he would have died without the operation? Should Alicia steal the money then?
7. Stealing is against the law. Which is more important—not breaking the law, or saving a human life?

# Religion or Medicine?

Perhaps you have seen stories in newspapers about families who refuse medical treatment because of their religion. Some people believe that diseases should not be treated by doctors or by medicine. They feel that all kinds of illness can be healed through faith. These people feel that the law gives them the right to live by their religion and depend on it for healing.

If an adult refuses medical treatment for himself or herself, doctors and hospitals usually do not object. However, when a parent refuses treatment for a child, the problem becomes more complicated.

Suppose that a child has been in an accident and has lost a lot of blood. The child has been brought to a hospital by people who saw the accident. The doctors there agree that the child will die in a few hours unless given blood. The parents are called, but they will not allow the blood to be given to their child. It is against their religion. The doctors argue that while the parents may refuse treatment for themselves, they do not have the right to keep needed medical help from another person, even if that person is their own child.

# Religion or Medicine?—Questions

1. What's the problem here?
2. Is it right for parents to refuse medical treatment for their children? Why or why not?
3. Suppose that one of the doctors asks a judge to write a court order saying that the parents must allow the injured child to be treated. Does the government (the judge) have the right to disregard the parents' wishes?
4. What if the child wants to be given blood but his or her parents won't allow it? Who should have the final say in this case—the child, or the parents?
5. What if the child does *not* want to be given blood and believes that faith can heal the injury?
6. What if the parents threaten to sue if the doctor gives the child the blood? Should this make any difference to the doctor?
7. When is it right to go against parents' wishes for their children?

# Dilemmas in Science and Current Events

Problems people face in the world around them.

# The Bowhead Whale

The Bowhead whale is in danger of becoming extinct. At the most, three thousand Bowheads are left in the world. They live in the Arctic Ocean. Russia, Japan, and the United States have all signed an agreement with the International Whaling Commission which says that they'll stop killing these whales.

Alaskan Eskimos set out each spring to kill and bring in Bowhead whales. This is a ritual, or ceremony, an important part of their culture, which began a long time ago when the Eskimos needed the Bowheads for food. Environmentalists argue that the Eskimos can now meet this need in other ways. They believe that even though Eskimos today use high-powered motor boats and modern hunting weapons, many whales are lost and left to die rather than being brought in.

The U.S. Government has asked the International Whaling Commission to go on letting the Eskimos hunt the Bowheads.

# The Bowhead Whale—Questions

1. What's the problem here?
2. Was it right or wrong for the United States to ask the whaling commission to let the Eskimos keep on killing the whales? Why?
3. The environmentalists have one point of view, and the Eskimos have another. The environmentalists believe that Bowheads should no longer be killed because they're nearly extinct. Once a species becomes extinct, it's gone forever. The Eskimos, on the other hand, have always hunted Bowheads for food. Hunting these whales is an important part of their culture. Which point of view is the right one? Why?
4. The United States asked that only Eskimos be allowed to hunt Bowheads—no one else. What about a poor Alaskan fishing village inhabited by white people? What if most of the people are unemployed and could use the money they'd make selling Bowhead whales? Should they be allowed to hunt them, too?
5. Is it important for human beings to worry about protecting animals from becoming extinct? If you think it is, give three reasons why. Which is the best reason?
6. Every year, during hunting season in the United States, people go out and shoot rabbits, deer, ducks, and other animals. None of these animals is in danger of becoming extinct, and each hunter is given a limit of how many he or she can kill. Most hunters hunt for sport—they don't really need to hunt for food. Is this right or wrong? Why?

# Skyjacking

Hijacking airplanes, or *skyjacking,* has happened often during the 1970's. In one year alone, there were sixty-two different tries to skyjack planes. Many skyjackers belong to terrorist political groups who hold the planes and passengers hostage for ransom demands. Sometimes they're successful. In September, 1977, the Japanese government gave five Japanese Red Army terrorists what they wanted so that the lives of 156 passengers could be saved.

Other skyjackings haven't been successful. In the famous raid on Entebbe airport in Uganda in July, 1976, Israeli soldiers rescued one hundred hostages who'd left Tel Aviv a few days before on their way to Paris. The skyjackers were German and Arab terrorists who supported the cause of the Arabs in Palestine. They held the passengers hostage and demanded that fifty-three other terrorists be released from jail. During the raid, all seven skyjackers were killed.

# Skyjacking—Questions

1. What are some of the problems that exist during a skyjacking?
2. What's the right way to deal with skyjackers—by giving in to their demands, like the Japanese did, or by risking a raid, like the Israeli soldiers did?
3. During the raid on Entebbe, not only the skyjackers were killed. Twenty Ugandan soldiers died, along with three hostages who were caught in the crossfire. Would it have made a difference if only the skyjackers had been killed and nobody else had been hurt?
4. Would it have made a difference if the skyjackers had killed any of the passengers during the skyjacking that led up to the Entebbe raid? Why or why not?
5. Is it any more right or wrong for soldiers to kill skyjackers than it is for skyjackers to kill hostages? Why?
6. Do you think that skyjackers should be executed after they're captured? Why or why not?
7. Sometimes skyjackers do what they do for political reasons. At other times, skyjackers are people who are mentally unbalanced. Is there any difference? If so, what?
8. Is it ever right to put a group of people in danger for any reason?

# Nuclear Power

The energy crisis is very real. Electricity and fuel shortages have caused prices to go up all over the world. In the Eastern United States, people have had to do without enough oil or natural gas for heating.

At one time, nuclear, or atomic, power plants seemed to be an answer to the energy shortage. Many people have questioned the safety of these plants, however. Critics of nuclear power say that these plants leak dangerous radioactivity and believe that cooling system breakdowns could cause disastrous explosions. They also say that nuclear power shouldn't be used because there's no safe way to get rid of the dangerous waste matter that is left over when power is made.

Imagine that people are talking about building a nuclear power plant in your town or city. You and your neighbors have been suffering from a power shortage for some time. The power plant would make enough electricity for everyone and would also provide workers with jobs.

# Nuclear Power—Questions

1. What's the problem here?
2. Should the power plant be built? Why or why not? What are the alternatives?
3. If your father had been out of work for a long time, and if he'd be able to get a job at the power plant, would this make a difference in your decision?
4. If your whole family had been sick last winter because the house hadn't been warm enough, would that make a difference?
5. Would the benefits of such a power plant outweigh the risks? Why or why not?
6. Safety regulations usually require that special evacuation plans be prepared for people who live within a certain distance from a nuclear power plant. If you lived within the most dangerous area, would that make a difference?
7. Harmful or poisonous chemicals are often transported from place to place by trains. Sometimes, these trains derail or have accidents. Whole towns have to be evacuated, and people exposed to the chemicals get very sick and some even die. Is there any difference between this type of situation and one involving a nuclear power plant? If so, what's the difference?

# Automobiles

Automobile exhaust accounts for much of the pollution in our cities. Because of this, many people believe that we should limit the use of automobiles and maybe even not allow them at all. They think that we should work on making more and better forms of public transportation, like trains, buses, and subways.

People who are against using automobiles also bring up the fact that nearly sixty thousand people die in car accidents each year, and four million more are injured. Besides all this, cars use up great amounts of natural resources, and the courts are always crowded with accident cases.

People who defend automobiles say that accidents, pollution, and other problems are the price we have to pay for the freedom, convenience, and comfort which our cars give us.

## Automobiles—Questions

1. What's the problem here?
2. Would it be right or wrong to set limits on how often people could drive their cars? Why? Would it be right or wrong to make it illegal for people to drive their cars? Why? What kinds of things would have to be considered before writing a law which bans cars?
3. Suppose that your family takes a vacation every year. You usually go far out into the country to camp—away from trains, buses, and subways. This year, your father says that your family can't take a vacation. He says that it's important to conserve gasoline. Would you think that this was fair? Why or why not?
4. Suppose that the government decides to limit the use of automobiles by placing a large tax on gasoline. In this way, people will buy less gas and drive their cars less often. Let's say that the tax on each gallon of gas would be fifty cents. A gallon of gas that cost seventy cents would then cost $1.20. Would this be a fair way to limit the use of cars? Why or why not? Who would be affected the most by gasoline tax?
5. Think of a fair way to limit the use of cars.

# Laetrile

You wouldn't think that apricot pits could cause arguments and problems, but they have. However, people are really arguing about a drug called Laetrile, which is made from crushed apricot pits. The people who sell and support the use of Laetrile say that the drug helps to prevent cancer, to treat cancer, and to relieve the pain of cancer.

Laetrile is not allowed in many states, yet thousands of people still use it. It's smuggled into the United States from other countries. The Food and Drug Administration won't allow Laetrile to be made in this country because the law says that people cannot use a new drug until it's been proved to work and be safe. While Laetrile hasn't been found to hurt anyone, no study has proved that it cures or prevents cancer. Officials of the American Cancer Society and the National Cancer Institute say that Laetrile is a fraud and believe that people who use Laetrile won't look for proper medical treatment. Most doctors don't think the drug should be used.

People who want Laetrile allowed say that since it doesn't hurt anyone there's no reason to stop people from using it if they want to. They feel that they have the right to choose how to be treated. They say that making Laetrile illegal limits their freedom of choice.

People who don't want Laetrile legalized feel that people who use it are only hurting themselves, and that those who sell it are taking advantage of others. They tell of cases in which people who've had a 65 percent chance of being cured by surgery have taken Laetrile instead and then died.

# Laetrile—Questions

1. What's the problem here?
2. Is it right or wrong to keep the use of Laetrile illegal? Why?
3. What's the best reason you can think of for keeping Laetrile illegal?
4. What's the best reason you can think of for making Laetrile legal?
5. Does the government have the right to ban things it thinks can harm people? Why or why not? Should people be able to make up their own minds in situations like these? Why or why not?
6. Many people feel that cigarettes and alcohol are harmful. Should these be made illegal? Why or why not? What do you think would happen if cigarettes and alcohol were made illegal?

# Basketballs and Pollution

Dresel Sports Equipment, Inc., is located in a small town. It's been making basketballs for many years and hires about two hundred workers who live in the town. During its operation, the company dumps dangerous chemicals and waste matter into the river which runs through the town. The river has become so polluted that the state government agency which works to protect the environment has sent an inspector, Ms. Smith, to look into the situation.

Ms. Smith has found that many fish are dying because of the pollution and that the water going to towns down the river has also become polluted. She's asked the company to stop polluting the river, but the owners are arguing that they can't because it would be too expensive to get rid of the wastes in any other way. They say that they'd have to go out of business if they had to follow the government antipollution requirements. A lot of workers would lose their jobs. The company also says that they can't even partly clean up the river unless they lay off ten to twenty workers to help pay for the cost of the cleanup.

# Basketballs and Pollution—Questions

1. What's the problem here?
2. Ms. Smith and her agency have the power and legal authority to force Dresel Sports Equipment to stop polluting. What do you think her decision should be? If she decides to force the company to stop polluting the river, then the company will either have to close or lay off some of its employees. Would either of these be right? Which would be more right? Why?
3. Suppose that the government offers to help Dresel Sports Equipment build a new nonpolluting factory. They'll have to get the money to do this by raising the taxes of the people who live in the town. Would this be right or wrong? Why?
4. What if your parents lived in the town, and their taxes would have to be raised? Would this make a difference to your decision? Why or why not? What if your father or mother worked for Dresel Sports?
5. What if Ms. Smith's father worked for Dresel Sports? Should this make a difference to her decision? Why or why not?
6. Write a law to deal with this situation fairly. Keep in mind that many people who live in the town work at Dresel Sports.

# Karen Quinlan

The Karen Quinlan case has been one of the most talked-about medical problems of the 1970's. Karen Quinlan was put into a hospital after becoming unconscious. The doctors found that her brain was damaged so badly that there was no hope of recovery. Special life-support equipment was used to keep her alive. When it became clear that her condition would never change, her parents asked that the life-support machines be disconnected. They argued that it was both unnatural and inhuman to keep Karen alive with machines when her life as a conscious human being had come to an end.

The hospital refused to either shut off the machines or let anyone else do it. They believed in using every possible means to keep Karen alive, no matter what her condition. They felt that stopping the machines would be the same as murdering her.

After a long legal battle, the New Jersey Supreme Court decided to allow the machines that were keeping Karen Quinlan alive to be turned off. When the machines were turned off, Karen started breathing on her own. She remained in a coma and was transferred to a nursing home. She has never regained consciousness.

# Karen Quinlan—Questions

1. What's the problem here?
2. Do you think that the New Jersey Supreme Court's decision was right or wrong? Why? What if Karen had died right after the machines had been turned off? Would that make a difference?
3. Suppose that someone like Karen regained consciousness but would always be paralyzed and need life-support equipment in order to stay alive. If that person insisted that he or she didn't want to live like that forever and wanted the equipment turned off, should the hospital grant his or her request?
4. What if the person's parents didn't want the equipment turned off? Who should have the final say?
5. Some people believe in *euthanasia,* or mercy killing. They think that a person who's suffering greatly, or who'll never recover from a terrible disease or accident, should be put out of his or her misery. Sometimes people who are very sick beg their relatives or their doctors to give them a shot or a drug that will help them to die. Is euthanasia right or wrong? Why?

# Gun Control

United States citizens who've never been convicted of serious crimes are allowed to own handguns. Whenever a person buys a handgun, his or her name is registered with the federal government, along with the serial number of the gun.

It's against the law to carry a gun in public or in a car if it's either loaded or hidden from sight. People can get permits to carry loaded or hidden guns, but these are generally given only under very special circumstances.

Because so many handguns are used in shootings and other crimes, a lot of people think that nobody should be allowed to own handguns. They point to facts like these to back up their arguments:

- 69 people are shot to death in the United States every day.
- 10,000 people use handguns to commit suicide every year.
- Half of all murders in the United States are done with handguns.

Those who believe that people should be allowed to own handguns argue that people need them in order to protect themselves.

## Gun Control—Questions

1. What's the problem here?
2. Would it be right or wrong to prohibit people from owning guns? Why?
3. Would it be right for anyone who wanted a gun to be allowed to own one? Why or why not?
4. Are there some kinds of people who shouldn't be allowed to own guns? Explain. Who has the right to make decisions like this? Why?
5. Should people be allowed to own anything they wish? Why or why not? Think of some things that U.S. citizens aren't allowed to own.
6. When does the government have the right to decide what people can and can't do?

# Appendix

## Definition of Kohlberg's Moral Stages

### I. Preconventional level

At this level, the child is responsive to cultural rules and labels of good and bad, right or wrong, but interprets these labels either in terms of the physical or the hedonistic consequences of action (punishment, reward, exchange of favors) or in terms of the physical power of those who enunciate the rules and labels. The level is divided into the following two stages:

Stage 1: *The punishment-and-obedience orientation.* The physical consequences of action determine its goodness or badness, regardless of the human meaning or value of these consequences. Avoidance of punishment and unquestioning deference to power are valued in their own right, not in terms of respect for an underlying moral order supported by punishment and authority (the latter being Stage 4).

Stage 2: *The instrumental-relativist orientation.* Right action consists of that which instrumentally satisfies one's own needs and occasionally the needs of others. Human relations are viewed in terms like those of the marketplace. Elements of fairness, of reciprocity, and of equal sharing are present, but they are always interpreted in a physical, pragmatic way. Reciprocity is a matter of "you scratch my back and I'll scratch yours," not of loyalty, gratitude, or justice.

### II. Conventional level

At this level, maintaining the expectations of the individual's family, group, or nation is perceived as valuable in its own right, regardless of immediate and obvious consequences. The attitude is not only one of *conformity* to personal expectations and social order, but of loyalty to it, of actively *maintaining,* supporting, and justifying the order, and of identifying with the persons or group involved in it. At this level, there are the following two stages:

Stage 3: *The interpersonal concordance or "good boy—nice girl"*
*orientation.* Good behavior is that which pleases or helps others and is approved by them. There is much conformity to stereotypical images of what is majority or "natural" behavior. Behavior is frequently judged by intention—"he means well" becomes important for the first time. One earns aporoval by being "nice."

Stage 4: *The "law and order" orientation.* There is orientation toward authority, fixed rules, and the maintenance of the social order. Right behavior consists of doing one's duty, showing respect for authority, and maintaining the given social order for its own sake.

### III. Postconventional, autonomous, or principled level

At this level, there is a clear effort to define moral values and principles that have validity and application apart from the authority of the groups or persons holding these principles and apart from the individual's own identification with these groups. This level also has two stages:

Stage 5: *The social-contract, legalistic orientation,* generally with utilitarian overtones. Right action tends to be defined in terms of general individual rights and standards which have been critically examined and agreed upon by the whole society. There is a clear awareness of the relativism of personal values and opinions and a corresponding emphasis upon procedural rules for reaching consensus. Aside from what is constitutionally and democratically agreed upon, the right is a matter of personal "values" and "opinion." The result is an emphasis upon the "legal point of view," but with an emphasis upon the possibility of changing law in terms of rational considerations of social utility (rather than freezing it in terms of Stage 4 "law and order"). Outside the legal realm, free agreement and contract is the binding element of obligation. This is the "official" morality of the American government and Constitution.

Stage 6: *The universal ethical-principle orientation.* Right is defined by the decision of conscience in accord with self-chosen *ethical principles* appealing to logical comprehensiveness, universality, and consistency. These principles are abstract and ethical (the Golden Rule, the categorical imperative); they are not concrete moral rules like the Ten Commandments. At heart, these are universal principles of *justice,* of the *reciprocity* and *equality* of human *rights,* and of respect for the dignity of human beings as *individual persons.*

Materials in Appendix used by permission of Lawrence Kohlberg.

# Piaget's Eras and Stages of Logical and Cognitive Development

### Era I (Age 0-2) Sensorimotor Intelligence
Stage 1—Reflex action.
Stage 2—Coordination of reflexes and sensorimotor repetition (primary circular reaction).
Stage 3—Activities to make interesting events in the environment reappear (secondary circular reaction).
Stage 4—Means/ends behavior and search for absent objects.
Stage 5—Experimental search for new means (tertiary circular reaction).
Stage 6—Use of imagery in insightful invention of new means and in recall of absent objects and events.

### Era II (Age 2-5) Symbolic, Intuitive, or Prelogical Thought
Inferences carried on through images and symbols that do not maintain logical relations or invariances with one another. "Magical thinking" is the sense of (a) confusion of apparent or imagined events with real events and objects and (b) confusion of perceptual appearances of qualitative and quantitative change with actual change.

### Era III (Age 6-10) Concrete Operational Thought
Inferences carried on through system of classes, relations, and quantities maintaining logically invariant properties and referring to concrete objects. Such logical processes are included as (a) lower-order classes in higher-order classes; (b) transitive seriation (recognition that if a $>$b and b$>$c, then a$>$c); (c) logical addition and multiplication of classes and quantities; (d) conservation of number, class membership, length, and mass under apparent change.
Substage 1: Formation of stable categorical classes.
Substage 2: Formation of quantitative and numerical relations of invariance.

### Era IV (Age 11-adulthood) Formal-Operational Thought
Inferences through logical operations upon propositions or "operations upon operations." Reasoning about reasoning. Construction of systems of all possible relations or implications. Hypothetical-deductive isolation of variables and testing of hypotheses.

Substage 1: Formation of the inverse of the reciprocal. Capacity to form negative classes (e.g., the class of all not-crows) and to see relations as simultaneously reciprocal (e.g., to understand that liquid in a U-shaped tube holds an equal level because of counterbalanced pressures).

Substage 2: Capacity to order triads of propositions or relations (e.g., to understand that if Bob is taller than Joe and Joe is shorter than Dick, then Joe is the shortest of the three).

Substage 3: True formal thought. Construction of all possible combinations of relations, systematic isolation of variables, and deductive hypothesis-testing.

# Relations* Between Piaget Logical Stages and Kohlberg Moral Stages

| Logical Stage | Moral Stage |
|---|---|
| Symbolic, intuitive thought | Stage 0: The good is what I want and like. |
| Concrete operations, Substage 1 Categorical classification | Stage 1: Punishment-obedience orientation. |
| Concrete operations, Substage 2 Reversible concrete thought | Stage 2: Instrumental hedonism and concrete reciprocity. |
| Formal operations, Substage 1 Relations involving the inverse of the reciprocal. | Stage 3: Orientation to interpersonal relations of mutuality. |
| Formal operations, Substage 2 | Stage 4: Maintenance of social order, fixed rules, and authority. |
| Formal operations, Substage 3 | Stage 5: Social Contract, utilitarian law-making perspective. |
| | Stage 6: Universal ethical principle orientation. |

*Attainment of the logical stages is necessary but not sufficient for attainment of the moral stage.

# Bibliography

Atkins, Victor S. "High School Students Who Teach: An Approach to Personal Learning." Ed.D dissertation, Harvard University School of Education, 1972.

Beck, Clive. "The Development of Moral Judgment." In *Developing Value Constructs in Schooling: Inquiry into Process and Product,* edited by J. A. Phillips, Jr. Worthington, Ohio: Ohio Association for Supervision and Curriculum Development, 1972.

Beyer, Barry K. "Conducting Moral Discussions in the Classroom." *Social Education,* April 1976.

Blatt, Moshe. "Studies on the Effects of Classroom Discussions upon Children's Moral Development." Ph.D. dissertation, University of Chicago, 1970.

Blatt, Moshe, and Kohlberg, Lawrence. "Studies on the Effects of Classroom Discussions upon Children's Moral Development." *Journal of Moral Education,* July 1975.

Burgess, Patricia. *Erica's School on the Hill.* Minneapolis, Minn.: Winston Press, 1979.

Byrne, Diane F. "The Development of Role-Taking in Adolescence." Ph.D. dissertation, Harvard University, 1973.

Colby, Anne. "Moral Change in Junior High Students." Ph.D. dissertation, Columbia University, 1972.

DeLapp, S. "Four Strategies to Encourage Evaluative Input from Children." *Insights into Open Education* 8 (1975):4-7.

Dewey, John. "The Need for a Philosophy of Education." In *John Dewey on Education: Selected Writings,* edited by R. Archambault. New York: Random House, 1964.

Doland, Dilman J., and Adelberg, Kathryn. "The Learning of Sharing Behavior." *Child Development* 38 (1967):695-700.

Dowell, Roland C. "Adolescents as Peer Counselors: A Program for Psychological Growth." Ed.D. dissertation, Harvard University School of Education, 1971.

Dulit, E. "Adolescent Thinking a la Piaget: The Formal Stage." *Journal of Youth and Adolescence* 1 (1972):281-301.

Elkind, David. *Children and Adolescents.* New York: Oxford University Press, 1972.

Erickson, V. Lois. "Psychological Growth for Women: A Cognitive-Developmental Curriculum Intervention." Ph.D. dissertation, University of Minnesota, 1973.

Erikson, E. H. "Identity and the Life Cycle." *Psychological Issues* 1 (1959).

Fenton, Edwin. "Moral Education: The Research Findings." *Social Education* (April 1976):188-93.

*First Things: Values.* Sound filmstrips for the primary years. Pleasantville, N.Y.: Guidance Associates, 1972.

Fraenkel, Jack R. *Helping Students Think and Value: Strategies for Teaching the Social Studies.* Englewood Cliffs, N.J.: Prentice-Hall, 1973.

Galbraith, Ronald E., and Jones, Thomas M. *Moral Reasoning: A Teaching Handbook for Adapting Kohlberg to the Classroom.* Anoka, Minn.: Greenhaven Press, 1976.

Galbraith, Ronald E., and Jones, Thomas M. "Teaching Strategies for Moral Dilemmas: An Application of Kohlberg's Theory to the Social Studies Classroom." *Social Education* 39 (January 1975):16-22.

Glasser, William. *Schools without Failure.* New York: Harper & Row, 1969.

Grimes, Patricia M. "Teaching Moral Reasoning to Eleven Year Olds and Their Mothers: A Means of Promoting Moral Development." Ed.D. dissertation, Boston University School of Education, 1972.

Hall, Robert T. *Moral Education: A Handbook for Teachers.* Minneapolis, Minn.: Winston Press, 1979.

Holstein, Constance B. "Moral Judgment in Early Adolescence and Middle Ages: A Longitudinal Study." Paper presented at the biennial meeting of the Society for Research in Child Development, 29 March-1 April 1973, Philadelphia, Pennsylvania.

Hophan, P. "A Project in Supporting Children's Thinking and Moral Development." Cortland, N.Y.: Project Change, SUNY at Cortland, 1975.

Kohl, H. *Thirty-six Children.* New York: New American Library, 1967.

Kohlberg, Lawrence. "The Cognitive-Developmental Approach to Moral Education." *Phi Delta Kappan* (June 1975):670-77.

Kohlberg, Lawrence. "A Concept of Developmental Psychology as the Central Guide to Education." In *Psychology and the Process of Schooling in the Next Decade,* edited by M. Reynolds. Minneapolis, Minn.: University of Minnesota Department of Audio-Visual Extension, 1972.

Kohlberg, Lawrence. "From Is to Ought: How to Commit the Naturalistic Fallacy and Get Away with It in the Study of Moral Development." In *Cognitive Development and Epistemology,* editied by T. Mischel. New York: Academic Press, 1971.

Kohlberg, Lawrence. "Humanistic and Cognitive-Developmental Perspectives on Psychological Education." In *Psychological Education: A Means to Promote Personal Development during Adolescence,* edited by R. Mosher and N. Sprinthall. Also in *The Counseling Psychologist* 2/4 (1971):3-82.

Kohlberg, Lawrence. "Stage and Sequence: The Cognitive-Developmental Approach to Socialization." In *Handbook of Socialization Theory and Research,* edited by D.A. Goslin. Chicago: Rand McNally, 1969.

Kohlberg, Lawrence, ed. *Collected Papers on Moral Development and Moral Education.* 2 vols. Cambridge: Harvard University Center for Moral Education, Laboratory of Human Development, 1973.

Kohberg, Lawrence, and Mayer, Rochelle. "Development as the Aim of Education." *Harvard Educational Review* 42 (1972):449-96.

Kohlberg, Lawrence; Fenton, Edwin; Speicher-Dubin, Betsy. "The Training of Teachers in Moral Education Techniques." In *Collected Tapes in Moral Education,* edited by L. Kohlberg, 1973.

Kohlberg, Lawrence; Colby, Anne; Fenton, Edwin; Speicher-Dubin, Betsy; and Lieberman, M. "Secondary School Moral Discussion Programs Led by Social Studies Teachers." In *Collected Papers,* edited by L. Kohlberg. Cambridge: Harvard Graduate School of Education, 1975.

Kur, J. "Using Small-Group Projects to Foster Cooperation in the Classroom." *Project Change Mini-Book on Fostering Moral Development in the Classroom.* Cortland, N.Y.: Project Change, SUNY at Cortland, Winter 1976.

Lengel, J. G. "Explanations of Developmental Change Applied to Education: Atmospheres for Moral Development." Educational Resources Information Center (ERIC), ED 104 738, 1974.

Lickona, Thomas. "The Challenge of Watergate to American Schools: Fostering the Moral Development of Children." Cortland, N.Y.: Project Change, SUNY at Cortland, 1976.

Lickona, Thomas. "Project Change: A Person-Centered Approach to Competency-based Teacher Educátion." *Journal of Teacher Education* 27 (1976):122-28.

Lickona, Thomas. "Teacher Approaches to Moral Education: An Interview and Observation Study." State University of New York at Cortland, 1976.

Loevinger, Jane, and Wessler, Ruth. *Measuring Ego Development.* 2 vols. San Francisco: Jossey-Bass, 1970.

Mackie, Peter A. "Teaching Counseling Skills to Low Achieving High School Students." Ed.D. dissertation, Boston University School of Education, 1974.

Mosher, Ralph L., and Sprinthall, Norman A. "Deliberate Psychological Education." *The Counseling Psychologist* 2/4 (1971):3-82.

Neill, Alexander S. *Summerhill: A Radical Approach to Child Rearing.* New York: Hart, 1960.

Paolitto, Diana. "Role-Taking Opportunities for Early Adolescents: A Program in Moral Education." Ed.D. dissertation, Boston University School of Education, 1975.

Piaget, Jean. *The Moral Judgment of the Child.* London: Routledge & Kegan Paul, 1932.

Raths, Louis E.; Harmin, Merrill; and Simon, Sidney B. *Values and Teaching.* Columbus, Ohio: Merrill, 1966.

Reimer, Joseph. "Moral Reasoning among Israeli Kibbutz Adolescents." Unpublished thesis, Harvard Graduate School of Education, 1977.

Rohwer, William J. "Prime Time for Education: Early Childhood or Adolescence?" *Harvard Educational Review* 41 (1971):316-41.

Scharf, Peter. *Moral Education.* Davis, Cal.: Responsible Action, 1978.

Scharf, Peter, ed. *Readings in Moral Education.* Minneapolis, Minn.: Winston Press, 1978.

Scharf, Peter, and Hickey, Joseph. *Towards a Just Community in Prison.* San Francisco: Jossey-Bass, 1979.

Selman, Robert L., and Jaquette, Dan. "To Understand and To Help: Implications of Developmental Research for the Education of Children with Interpersonal Problems." In *Readings in Moral Education,* edited by Peter Scharf. Minneapolis, Minn.: Winston Press, 1978.

Sprinthall, Norman A. "Humanism: A New Bag of Virtues for Guidance?" *Personnel and Guidance Journal* 50 (1972):346-49.

Sprinthall, Norman A., and Mosher, Ralph L. "Voices from the Back of the Classroom." *Journal of Teacher Education* 22 (1971):166-75.

Stanley, S. "A Curriculum to Affect the Moral Atmosphere of the Family and the Moral Development of Adolescents." Ed.D. dissertation, Boston University School of Education, 1975.

Sullivan, Harry Stack. *The Interpersonal Theory of Psychiatry.* New York: Norton, 1953.

Thrower, Joan. "Moral Reasoning among Institutionalized Orphan Children." Unpublished thesis, Harvard Graduate School of Education, 1972.

Turiel, Elliot. "An Experimental Analysis of Developmental Stages in the Child's Moral Judgment." *Journal of Personality and Social Psychology,* 1966.

# Index of Dilemmas